CREATIVE BROODING

Creative Brooding

Robert A. Raines

Collier Books
A Division of Macmillan Publishing Co., Inc.
New York

Collier Macmillan Publishers
London

Macmillan Publishing Co., Inc.
866 Third Avenue, New York, N.Y.   10022
Collier Macmillan Canada, Ltd.

Library of Congress Cataloging in Publication Data
Raines, Robert Arnold, ed.
     Creative brooding.
     1. Devotional literature. I. Title.
BV4801.R3 1977   242   77-22181
ISBN 0-02-081200-0

First Collier Books Edition 1977

Creative Brooding is also published in a hardcover edition by Macmillan Publishing Co., Inc.

Printed in the United States of America

The author wishes to thank the following for permission to reproduce copyrighted material: *The New York Times* for "The Brass Rail Communion Table" by Gay Talese, © 1964 by The New York Times Company; "The Face of My Secret Heart" by Russell Baker, © 1964; "Observer: The Ubiquity of Fun or Stop the Music" by Russell Baker, © 1964 by The New York Times Company; and "What's Your Disguise" by Gay Talese, © 1965 by The New York Times Company. Reprinted by permission. *Look* for "Memo About a Dallas Citizen," Copyright 1964 by Cowles Broadcasting, Inc. Harper & Row for "Letter from Birmingham Jail"—April 16, 1963—from pp. 83-84 in *Why We Can't Wait* by Martin Luther King, Jr. Copyright © 1963 by Martin Luther King, Jr. *Pennsylvania Law Enforcement Journal* for "a letter written by a boy." Sterling Lord Agency for *The Detached Americans* by John Keats, Copyright 1965 John Keats. Charles Scribner's Sons for *Meditations for a Young Boy Confirmed* by Alan Paton, reprinted by permission of Charles Scribner's Sons. Copyright 1954 Alan Paton. *Satur-*

For
CATHARINE, BARBARA, *and* NANCY—
our creative brood

I want to thank those who have **helped** me in the writing of this book. I am grateful to Clement Alexandre, who encouraged the writing of such a book and gave valuable suggestions throughout its preparation; Joan Hemenway and Dick Raines, whose comments on the manuscript improved it; Virginia Hamilton, who typed draft upon draft with constant goodwill and patience; Peggy Raines, who helped select many of the pieces and whose good judgment helped bring the book to its final form.

I thank those human beings, ancient and contemporary, whose searching spirits breathe fresh life into me from these pages of their lives.

My own need for creative brooding grows: in order that I may savor solitude and become centered in my self, reach out to share community and work for justice in the world.

Kirkridge, Bangor, Pa.   *Robert A. Raines*
July 1977

Contents

CREATIVE BROODING

Introduction

RUSSELL BAKER writes, "The number of places where a person can escape entertainment becomes smaller every year.... It used to be, for example, that a man could go to his dentist and count on an undisturbed bout of suffering which helped him to grasp the transience of life and perceive the agony of the flesh. No longer. Nowadays, while the drill bites at his nerve ends, he will be entertained by an invisible orchestra playing 'The March of the Wooden Soldiers' through a hole in the ceiling. This invisible orchestra is spreading across the country like the chestnut blight. It hounds people at the supermarket with 'The Skater's Waltz,' deadens the air of cocktail lounges with 'Old Folks at Home,' and drips 'Giannina Mia' over lunch.... A people forced to live with Leonard Bernstein in the elevator, Doris Day at 30,000 feet, and 'The Animals' on the commuter bus is a people that will have precious little to smile about at the end of a hard day's entertainment. To restore entertainment to its proper role in society, we must restore the right to brood undisturbed."[1]

With all the important rights being defended these days, no group of aroused citizens is lobbying for the right to brood undisturbed. It's a pity. Why should we let ourselves be entertained right out of our minds without putting up a fight? Halford Luccock once said that in today's televised world we are all going to have eyes the size of cantaloupes and brains the size of split peas. *Something* is splitting in our heads, and a little brooding undisturbed may be just what the doctor ordered.[2]

Unfortunately the word *brooding* has a bad image these days. It connotes a low-grade distemper, meditative melancholy, the power of negative thinking. But this is unfair to *brooding,* which, as any hen knows, can be a most productive experience. It's the sort of "sitting on an idea" that often yields fresh insight. It's the kind of fruitful pondering a man may do in the solitude of early morning or late evening, or when protected by the anonymity of a commuter train or bus. We may regret the fact that there aren't many ideal brooding places left in our metropolitan milieu. (Who can brood undisturbed on the subway, in the kitchen—Brother Lawrence didn't have children—in front of a machine or in a busy office?) Yet, creative brooding depends as much on what's going on *inside* you as *around* you. An idea or person or event comes to mind and solicits your attention. You stop whatever you're doing for a moment —wherever you happen to be—and begin to *reflect*.

Kierkegaard, the intellectual's brooder par excellence, wrote in his journal one day in 1847: "Reflections . . . must not so much move, mollify, reassure, persuade as *awaken* and provoke men and sharpen thought. The time of reflections is indeed prior to action, and their purpose therefore is to rightly set all the elements into motion. Reflections ought to be a gadfly; therefore their tone ought to be quite different from that of edifying discourse, which rests in mood, but reflections ought in the good sense to be impatient, high-spirited in mood. Irony is necessary here and the even more significant ingredient of the comic. One may well laugh once in a while, if only to make the thought clearer and more striking. . . . Therefore, the reflections must . . . fetch [men] up out of the cellar, call to them, turn their comfortable way of thinking topsy-turvy with the dialectic of truth."[3]

Wouldn't it be intriguing to collect stories, quotations, human dramas from all kinds of sources that would set us to reflecting like that! Reflections in the depths where foundations are shaken, fear rises up, and hope is born. Gadfly reflections to awaken thought and precipitate action.

I began to reflect on the idea of making such a collection. Slowly it dawned on me that the result would constitute a kind of devotional book. With this realization my feet grew cold and my hands clammy. Don't misunderstand. I have no wish to disparage "devotional" books. But I have to confess that most such books or pamphlets are of little help to me personally. I am reminded of the comment of a friend, a Roman Catholic priest, who was describing the experience of hearing the confessions of nuns. He said, "It's like being stoned to death with popcorn." Much devotional material (unlike the devoted lives of nuns) is so much pious popcorn—fluffy, weightless, and stale.

This book, therefore, is not intended to comfort, reassure, or in the usual sense of the term, inspire. It is intended in Kierkegaardian fashion to provoke thought and trigger action. It is not intended for those who have no more questions. It *is* intended for those who must say every day of their lives, "I believe, help my unbelief."[4] It *is* intended for those who are willing to confront the truth in the grace of life and to seek meaning more in what is problematic than in what is pleasant.

The daily format typically includes a reflection, two or three Biblical passages, and a brief prayer or comment. Each daily reflection is a human drama or statement taken from the newspaper, a contemporary play, novel, or other writing. The reflections are not arranged in any particular order or according to any over-all design. They were not chosen because they were embedded in "great literature"—though some of them are —but because they hearken to great longings, indignations, and loves hidden in the depths of our being. They speak our language. If they have any common mark, it is the authentic humanity which breathes through their belief or unbelief. You will discover the Word of God coming to you out of strange mouths, though nothing perhaps so strange as happened to Balaam many years ago.[5] You will recognize yourself in these dramas and, hopefully, be provoked to creative brooding.

Following the daily reflection there is a Biblical selection. It is *not* there to "answer" a question raised in the reflection, as though the Bible were an answer book for human problems. In fact, the Bible questions *us* more than it answers our questions, as Job discovered. So do not expect neat, tidy Biblical assurances here; but rather, expect to be apprehended, exposed, and summoned by these passages. Each passage was chosen because it expresses the same question or concern embodied in the reflection to which it is attached. The same Spirit blows through both. The passages help us to recognize that the Word addressed to us in the "worldly" reflection is the same Word that confronts us in the Bible.

Meet the Word in the words, and let the Word in the words meet you. Wrestle with God, struggle with Him.[6] It is better to offend Him than to ignore Him; better to embrace Him than to tip your hat to Him. And get ready to be taken by surprise as day after day these words put the finger on some secret you thought no one else knew about or could possibly understand. Martin Buber said that real self-knowledge leads a person either to self-destruction or to rebirth.[7] In any genuine encounter with God the stakes are no less. It's a fearful and wonderful thing to fall into the hands of the living God,[8] and that just *could* happen to you as you reflect and respond.

Following the Biblical selection there is a brief prayer or comment. It is there to focus a main thrust of the reflection and/or the passage. It may carry the weight of your own hope or fear. If so, let it be like the end of a line, the other end of which is in the hand of God.[9] Or perhaps the prayer will be miles away from that thought which has risen within you. If so, forget it and think your own thought in the realization that God

[4]

understands the sighs too deep for words and "loves what is left over at the bottom of your heart."[10]

Creative brooding produces action. So get ready every day to open a door[11] or pound on one,[12] to withhold a word[13] or speak one,[14] to defer a visit[15] or make one,[16] to render an apology[17] or have a party,[18] to see a vision, dream a dream.[19] *Répondez, s'il vous plaît!* Sing a song;[20] jump over a wall![21]

SOME SUGGESTIONS

1. Resist the temptation to skim quickly through all the reflections.
2. Reserve a daily time and place for reflection. Only "unfree men are horrified by the suggestion of accepting a daily discipline. Confusing inner control with external tyranny, they prefer caprice to self-restraint."[22] Somewhere in your day there is a time for reflection, as for everything else.[23] Find it; enjoy it.
3. Have a Bible handy to read "around" the passages listed.

REFERENCES

1. Russell Baker, "Observer: The Ubiquity of Fun or Stop the Music," The New York *Times,* Dec. 15, 1964, p. 420.
2. Mark 6:31. "...Come with me by yourselves to some lonely place where you can rest quietly."
3. Soren Kierkegaard, *Works of Love,* Harper Torchbooks, Harper & Row, New York, 1962, translator's introduction, p. 12, note 2.
4. Mark 9:24.
5. Numbers 22–25 (especially 22)
6. Genesis 32:22–31
7. Martin Buber, *I and Thou,* Charles Scribner's Sons, New York, 1958, p. 64.
8. Hebrews 10:31 via Jonathan Edwards
9. See Abraham Joshua Heschel, *Man's Quest for God,* Charles Scribner's Sons, New York, 1954, p. 30.
10. Heschel, *Man's Quest for God,* p. 40, note 17
11. Revelations 3:20

12. Luke 11:5-10
13. Matthew 7:1
14. Acts 9:10-17; see 9:17
15. Romans 15:22
16. Acts 10; see 10:23
17. Matthew 5:23, 24
18. Luke 14:1-24
19. Joel 2:28; see Acts 2:17
20. Psalm 96:1. "O sing to the Lord a new song; sing to the Lord, all the earth."
21. Psalm 18:29. "Yea, by thee I can crush a troop; and by my God I can leap over a wall."
22. Abraham Joshua Heschel, *Man's Quest for God,* Charles Scribner's Sons, New York, 1954, p. 93.
23. Ecclesiastes 3:1-11

I *I Am Not an Exceptional Man*

ARNOLD, who has made his no-questions-asked peace with the world for $30,000 a year, speaks to his ne'er-do-well brother Murray, who has rebelled against the deceits of conventional society and cares about people passionately.

I have long been aware, Murray. . . . I have long been aware that you don't respect me much. I suppose there are a lot of brothers who don't get along. . . . Unfortunately for you, Murray, you want to be a hero. Maybe if a fella falls into a lake, you can jump in and save him; there's still that kind of stuff. But who gets opportunities like that in midtown Manhattan, with all that traffic? I am willing to deal with the available world and I do not choose to shake it up but to live with it. There's the people who spill things, and the people who get spilled on; I do not choose to notice the stains, Murray. I have a wife and two children, and business, like they say, is business. I am not an exceptional man, so it is possible for me to stay with things the way they are. I'm lucky, I'm gifted; I have a talent for surrender. I'm at peace. But you are cursed, and I like you, so it makes me sad, you don't have the gift; and I see the torture of it. All I can do is worry for you. But I will not worry for myself; you cannot convince me that I am one of the Bad Guys. I get up, I go, I lie a little, I peddle a little, I watch the rules, I talk the talk. We fellas have those offices high up there so we can watch the wind and go with it, however it blows. But, and I will not apologize for it, I take pride; I am the best possible Arnold Burns.

—*Herb Gardner,* playwright

[7]

Every one deceives his neighbor,
    and no one speaks the truth;
They have taught their tongue to speak lies;
    they commit iniquity and are too weary to repent.
                        —Jeremiah 9:5

"... from the least to the greatest
    every one is greedy for unjust gain;
from prophet to priest
    every one deals falsely.
They have healed the wound of my people lightly,
    saying, 'Peace, peace,'
    when there is no peace.
Were they ashamed when they committed abomination?
    No, they were not at all ashamed;
    they did not know how to blush.
Therefore they shall fall among the fallen;
    when I punish them, they shall be overthrown,"
                          says the Lord.
                    —Jeremiah 8:10b–12

Whoever cares for his own safety is lost; but if a man
will let himself be lost for my sake and for the Gospel,
that man is safe. What does a man gain by winning the
whole world at the cost of his true self? What can he
give to buy that self back?
                    —Mark 8:35 (NEB)

O God make me discontent with things the way they are
       in the world,
       and in my **own** life.
Teach me how to blush again,
       for the tawdry deals,
           the arrogant-but-courteous prejudice,
           the snickers,
           the leers,

the good food and drink which make me
too weary to repent,
the flattery given and received,
my willing use of rights and privileges
other men are unfairly denied.
Make me notice the stains when people get spilled on.
Make me care about the slum child downtown,
the misfit at work,
the people crammed into the
mental hospital,
the men, women, and youth
behind bars.
Jar my complacence; expose my excuses; get me involved
in the life of my city,
and give me integrity once more.

I see my son is wearing long trousers, I tremble at this;
I see he goes forward confidently, he does not know
    so fully his own gentleness.
Go forward, eager and reverent child, see here I begin
    to take my hands away from you,
I shall see you walk careless on the edges of the precipice,
    but if you wish you shall hear no word come out
    of me;
My whole soul will be sick with apprehension, but
    I shall not disobey you.
Life sees you coming, she sees you come with assurance
    towards her,
She lies in wait for you, she cannot but hurt you;
Go forward, go forward, I hold the bandages and oint-
    ments ready,
And if you would go elsewhere and lie alone with
    your wounds, why I shall not intrude upon you,
If you would seek the help of some other person, I
    shall not come forcing myself upon you.
If you should fall into sin, innocent one, that is the
    way of this pilgrimage;
Struggle against it, not for one fraction of a moment
    concede its dominion.
It will occasion you grief and sorrow, it will torment
    you,
But hate not God, nor turn from Him in shame or
    self-reproach;
He has seen many such, His compassion is as great as
    His Creation.
Be tempted and fall and return, return and be tempted
    and fall

A thousand times and a thousand, even to a thousand
thousand.
For out of this tribulation there comes a peace, deep
in the soul, and surer than any dream. . . .

—*Alan Paton,* author

When Israel was a child, I loved him,
and out of Egypt I called my son.
The more I called them,
The more they went from me. . . .
Yet it was I too taught Ephraim to walk,
I took them up in my arms;
but they did not know that I healed them.
I led them with cords of compassion,
with bands of love,
and I became to them as one
who eases the yoke on their jaws,
and I bent down to them and fed them.

—*Hosea 11:1-4*

Or what man of you, if his son asks him for a loaf,
will give him a stone? Or if he asks for a fish, will
give him a serpent?

If you, then, who are evil, know how to give good
gifts to your children, how much more will your
Father who is in heaven give good things to those
who ask him?

-Matthew 7:7-11

Lord, it's so hard to let my children go,
    to life, to suffering, to you.
It's so hard to leave my friends alone
    to work out their own problems.
Help me to trust more, and interfere less.

I give them over to you, Lord.
    Bend down to them,
      take care of them,
        give good things to them.

3 *The Brass Rail Communion Table*

It was the sort of West Side bar that even a libel lawyer would call a "dive." The stools were patched, the neon light was cracked, the drinkers seemed tired, dusty and lonely—like the neighborhood. And yet the blonde girl behind the bar did not fit the scene at all. She possessed a just-bathed look and was obviously intelligent and very polite and cheerful. When the other barmaids would steal her tips, she would not complain; when one of the men at the bar would become insulting, she would seem not to hear.

The owner of the bar could never understand why she had applied in June for employment in such a place. He did not know . . . that she was a University of California graduate in sociology, and that the $90-a-week summer job behind the bar was part of her "course" in the study of the drinker, the decadent neighborhood, and its effect upon loneliness.

He was not upset, just dumbfounded when Astrid Huerter told him this. And he was astonished too, when she said the employment there had been "very educational." Later Miss Huerter, a 21-year-old native of Germany who got a scholarship to study in this country, said that many of her preconceived notions of life in a "dive" had proved to be false. There is a kind of "morality" to be found there, she said, and many of the regular drinkers, some of them derelicts, soon began to worry about her, to wonder what "a nice girl like you" is doing in such a place.

"A few of them said they knew of other jobs for me that weren't so 'low class,'" she said. "They wanted to rescue me—they who could barely help themselves." Most of the regular patrons, she said, came to the bar not out of a need to drink or to pass the time of night; they came rather "out of a desperate need to communicate with someone and a desire to be heard." If it was merely alcohol that they wanted, they could have got it at half the price from a liquor store; and if they wished merely to pass the time, they could have gone to the movies. . . . But only in the neighborhood bar . . . could they be certain of being heard and that was her job there—professional listener. . . . "In New York . . . people do not have time to listen. Here everything is 'getting ahead' and 'progress'—and 'money.' Here you have to pay people to listen. And that is what a barmaid does."

—Gay Talese, journalist

. . . for I was hungry and you gave me food; I was thirsty and you gave me drink; and I was a stranger and you welcomed me.

—Matthew 25:35

. . . he saw a tax-gatherer, Levi by name, at his seat in the custom-house. He said to him, "Follow me"; and he rose to his feet, left everything behind, and followed him.

Afterwards Levi held a big reception in his house for Jesus; among the guests were a large party of tax-gatherers and others. The Pharisees and the lawyers of their sect complained to his disciples: "Why do you eat and drink," they said, "with tax-gatherers and sinners?" Jesus answered them: "It is not the healthy that need a doctor, but the sick."

—Luke 5:27-31 (NEB)

One of the Pharisees invited him to dinner; he went to the Pharisee's house and took his place at table.

A woman who was living an immoral life in the town had learned that Jesus was dining in the Pharisee's house and had brought oil of myrrh in a small flask. She took her place behind him, by his feet, weeping. His feet were wetted with her tears and she wiped them with her hair, kissing them and anointing them with the myrrh. When his host the Pharisee saw this he said to himself, "If this fellow were a real prophet, he would know who this woman is that touches him, and what sort of woman she is, a sinner." Jesus took him up and said, "Simon, I have something to say to you."

"Speak on, Master," said he. "Two men were in debt to a money-lender: one owed him five hundred silver pieces, the other fifty. As neither had anything to pay with he let them both off. Now, which will love him most?" Simon replied, "I should think the one that was let off most." "You are right," said Jesus. Then turning to the woman, he said to Simon, "You see this woman? I came to your house: you provided no water for my feet; but this woman has made my feet wet with her tears and wiped them with her hair. You gave me no kiss; but she has been kissing my feet ever since I came in. You did not anoint my head with oil; but she has anointed my feet with myrrh. And so, I tell you, her great love proves that her many sins have been forgiven; where little has been forgiven, little love is shown."

—*Luke 7:36–47* (NEB)

And he took a cup. . . . And he took bread. . . .
—*Luke 22:17,19*

I am ashamed, Lord.
You know how I look down on people

who don't live the way I think they should.
You see my frowns,
You hear my condemnations,
You watch my scorn tearing people down.
Forgive me.

Help me to accept my family,
                    my next-door neighbors,
                    my colleagues,
                    and myself,
    as Jesus accepted Levi, Simon, and the Woman,
    as you accept us all.

Thank you for listening to me.
Make me a listener.

4 *What Do I Care?*

PLAYBOY: Are you a socialist yourself?

MASTROIANNI: I'm the son of workers. What else could I be? I'll admit I'm a rose-water socialist—that is, I'm not active. I don't belong to the party and I avoid involvement, because it means compromise. So I stand in the window and watch....

PLAYBOY: Many movie marriages wind up on the rocks. Why has yours lasted?

MASTROIANNI: I've accepted my wife's defects and she's accepted mine. This is out of sufferance and I suppose because we're modern about it. It's useless to try and escape ourselves. Maybe we're not ideal together, but maybe we are. We're both full of defects, many defects. Maybe we weren't made to be together; but for this very reason it might be too easy *not* to stay together. So we say, "Let's stick it out all the same." It's a kind of game we want to make work.

PLAYBOY: Does your Catholicism have anything to do with why you remain married?

MASTROIANNI: No, I'm not a real Catholic, anyway —even though I *am* religious. Jesus Christ is an admirable example, but he's too remote from men of today to be a model. Or he's too much of one to be understood and followed. A man who dies for others is moving and admirable, but how many followers can he have in a world filled with people who will hardly help you across the street, let alone die for you?

PLAYBOY: You believe in a life after death?

MASTROIANNI: Truthfully, no. If I did, life would be more noble, more interesting, because it would have an ultimate goal—that of continuing. If I were a profound Catholic and believed in the afterlife of the

[17]

soul, I'd be a man of greater force and more clear-minded, because I'd have a precise purpose to prepare myself for. But since I fear everything will end in death, I say, "What do I care?"

—*Marcello Mastroianni,* actor

For the living know that they will die, but the dead know nothing, and they have no more reward; but the memory of them is lost. Their love and their hate and their envy have already perished, and they have no more for ever any share in all that is done under the sun. Go, eat your bread with enjoyment, and drink your wine with a merry heart. . . . The race is not to the swift, nor the battle to the strong, nor bread to the wise, nor riches to the intelligent, nor favor to the men of skill; but time and chance happen to them all. For man does not know his time. Like fish which are taken in an evil net, and like birds which are caught in a snare, so the sons of men are snared at an evil time, when it suddenly falls upon them.

—*Ecclesiastes 9:5–7a,11,12*

And he told them a parable, saying, "The land of a rich man brought forth plentifully; and he thought to himself, 'What shall I do, for I have nowhere to store my crops?' And he said, 'I will do this: I will pull down my barns, and build larger ones; and there I will store all my grain and my goods. And I will say to my soul, Soul, you have ample goods laid up for many years; take your ease, eat, drink, and be merry.'

But God said to him, 'Fool! This night your soul is required of you; and the things you have prepared, whose will they be? . . .' "

—*Luke 12:16–20*

I stand in the window and watch most of the time,
   and admire Jesus Christ from a distance,
   a safe distance.
I like to take things easy and enjoy life, Lord.
Am I a fool?
Why does that phrase "what do I care?" bother me?
   I *do* care about justice in this country,
   and happiness in my family,
   and faith in you, Lord.

Make me care enough to commit myself,
   and get involved.

5 *Call Me Eccentric*

When narcotics squad detectives recently raided a loft apartment in a depressed area of New York City, they came on a scene straight out of "The Beggar's Opera." Every square foot of the long, dingy apartment was crowded with human derelicts who were sleeping on the floor, or sitting huddled in corners; dimly visible overhead were a number of gay paper ceiling ornaments, left over from the days when the loft had been a dance hall. After searching the crowd, the detectives arrested six men who were carrying hypodermic needles and packets of heroin; they also arrested the derelicts' host, a mild, weedy-looking man who was charged with harboring drug addicts in his apartment.

At police headquarters, the weedy-looking man claimed he was actually well-to-do, but that he had chosen to live among the homeless in order to provide them with food, shelter, and clothing. His door, he said, was open to all, including a small minority of narcotic addicts, since he had not known it was against the law to feed and clothe people with the drug habit. Checking his story, the police found that the man was indeed neither a vagrant nor a drug addict. He was John Sargent Cram, a millionaire who had been educated at Princeton and Oxford and whose family had long been noted for its philanthropies. Wishing to avoid the rigmarole of organized charity work, Cram had simply moved into the loft and set about helping the derelicts directly, at a cost of $100 or so a day. He made a point of not giving the men money, he told the police, because it only went for cheap wine.

At a later hearing, a variety of witnesses spoke of Cram's kindness and altruism, and it was brought out that the Spanish-speaking population of the area knew him as Papa Dio—"Father God." Amid cheers in the courtroom, the Prince Myshkin-like Mr. Cram was freed on his promise that he would bar drug addicts from his loft. He later told reporters, "I don't know that my work does much good, but I don't think it does any harm. I'm quite happy, you know. I'm anything but a despondent person. Call me eccentric. Call it my reason for being. I have no other."

—Hallowell Bowser, editor

. . . we have become a spectacle to the world. . . . We are fools for Christ's sake. . . .

—I Corinthians 4:9,10

It is by this that we know what love is: that Christ laid down his life for us. And we in turn are bound to lay down our lives for our brothers. But if a man has enough to live on, and yet when he sees his brother in need shuts up his heart against him, how can it be said that the divine love dwells in him? My children, love must not be a matter of words or talk; it must be genuine, and show itself in action.

—I John 3:16–18 (NEB) *and see also*
Matthew 25:31–46

Let your bearing towards one another arise out of your life in Christ Jesus. For the divine nature was his from the first; yet he did not think to snatch at equality with God, but made himself nothing, assuming the nature of a slave. Bearing the human likeness, revealed in human shape, he humbled himself, and in obedience accepted even death—death on a cross. Therefore God raised him to the heights and bestowed on him the name above all names, that at the name of Jesus every knee should bow—in heaven, on earth, and in the depths—and every tongue confess "Jesus Christ is Lord," to the glory of God the Father.

So you too, my friends, must be obedient, as always; even more, now that I am away, than when I was with you. You must work out your own salvation in fear and trembling; for it is God who works in you, inspiring both the will and the deed, for his own chosen purpose.

—Philippians 2:5–13 (NEB)

Lord, you were a fool for my sake.
  Give me the guts to be a fool for your sake;
  to take a job where I can serve people
    more directly,
  to associate with all kinds of people in
    working for fair housing,
              better public education,
              a healthy two-party system,
  to spend my time and money for the
  poor, the sick, the forgotten, the undesirable . . .
  and to do these things whether or not
    my relatives and friends think I'm foolish.

Lord, keep me from being a damn fool,
  but let me be a fool for your sake.

6   *Who Am I?*

Who am I? They often tell me
I would step from my cell's confinement
calmly, cheerfully, firmly,
like a squire from his country-house.

Who am I? They often tell me
I would talk to my warders
freely and friendly and clearly,
as though it were mine to command.

Who am I? They also tell me
I would bear the days of misfortune
equably, smilingly, proudly,
like one accustomed to win.

Am I then really all that which other men tell of?
Or am I only what I know of myself,
restless and longing and sick, like a bird in a cage,
struggling for breath, as though hands were compressing
   my throat,
yearning for colours, for flowers, for the voices of birds,
thirsting for words of kindness, for neighbourliness,
trembling with anger at despotisms and petty humiliation,
tossing in expectation of great events,
powerlessly trembling for friends at an infinite distance,
weary and empty at praying, at thinking, at making,
faint, and ready to say farewell to it all?

Who am I? This or the other?
Am I one person today, and tomorrow another?
Am I both at once? A hypocrite before others,
and before myself a contemptibly woebegone weakling?
Or is something within me still like a beaten army,
fleeing in disorder from victory already achieved?

Who am I? They mock me, these lonely questions of mine
Whoever I am, thou knowest, O God, I am thine.
—*Dietrich Bonhoeffer,* theologian

As a hart longs
   for flowing streams,
so longs my soul
   for thee, O God.
My soul thirsts for God,
   for the living God.
When shall I come and behold
   the face of God? ...

Why are you cast down, O my soul,
   and why are you disquieted within me?
Hope in God; for I shall again praise him,
   my help and my God.
—*Psalm 42:1, 2, 5*

Now we see only puzzling reflections in a mirror,
   but then we shall see face to face.
My knowledge now is partial; then it will be
   whole, like God's knowledge of me.
—*I Corinthians 13:12*

I am thine, save me.
—*Psalm 119:94*

Lord, I do not know myself,
   but you know me.
I am ashamed that you know me.
   How can you love me?

Yet you *do* love me. Thank you!
Thank you for accepting me,
                understanding me,
                forgiving me.

Whatever I am worth to you,
                I am yours.

7 *The Singers of Life*

ONE DAY Loren Eiseley leaned against a stump at the edge of a small glade and fell asleep.

When I awoke, dimly aware of some commotion and outcry in the clearing, the light was slanting down through the pines in such a way that the glade was lit like some vast cathedral. I could see the dust motes of wood pollen in the long shaft of light, and there on the extended branch sat an enormous raven with a red and squirming nestling in his beak. The sound that awoke me was the outraged cries of the nestling's parents, who flew helplessly in circles about the clearing. The sleek black monster was indifferent to them. He gulped, whetted his beak on the dead branch a moment and sat still. Up to that point the little tragedy had followed the usual pattern. But suddenly, out of all that area of woodland, a soft sound of complaint began to rise. Into the glade fluttered small birds of half a dozen varieties drawn by the anguished outcries of the tiny parents.

No one dared to attack the raven. But they cried there in some instinctive common misery. The bereaved and the unbereaved. The glade filled with their soft rustling and their cries. They fluttered as though to point their wings at the murderer. There was a dim intangible ethic he had violated, that they knew. He was a bird of death. And he, the murderer, the black bird at the heart of life, sat on there, glistening in the common light, formidable, unmoving, unperturbed, untouchable.

The sighing died. It was then I saw the judgment. It was the judgment of life against death. I will never see it again so forcefully presented. I will never hear it again in notes so tragically prolonged. For in the midst of protest, they forgot the violence. There, in that clearing, the crystal note of a song sparrow lifted hesitantly in the hush. And finally, after painful fluttering, another took the song, and then another, the song passing from one bird to another, doubtfully at first, as though some evil thing were being slowly forgotten. Till suddenly they took heart and sang from many throats joyously together as birds are known to sing. They sang because life is sweet and sunlight beautiful. They sang under the brooding shadow of the raven. In simple truth they had forgotten the raven, for they were the singers of life, and not of death.

—*Loren Eiseley,* anthropologist

. . . though I walk through the valley of the
    shadow of death,
  I fear no evil;
for thou art with me. . . .
Thou preparest a table before me
  in the presence of my enemies. . .

—*Psalm 23:4,5* (incomplete)

I consider that the sufferings of this present time are not worth comparing with the glory that is to be revealed to us. For the creation waits with eager longing for the revealing of the sons of God; for the creation was subjected to futility, not of its own will but by the will of him who subjected it in hope; because the creation itself will be set free from its bondage to decay and obtain the glorious liberty of the children of God. We know that the whole creation has been groaning in travail together until now; and not only the creation, but we ourselves, who have the first fruits of the Spirit, groan inwardly as we wait for adoptions as sons, the redemption of our bodies. For in this hope we were saved. Now hope that is seen is not hope. For who hopes for what he sees? But if we hope for what we do not see, we wait for it with patience. Likewise the Spirit helps us in our weakness; for we do not know how to pray as we ought, but the Spirit himself intercedes for us with sighs too deep for words. . . .

What then shall we say to this? If God is for us, who is against us? He who did not spare his own Son, but gave him up for us all, will he not also give us all things with him? . . . Who shall separate us from the love of Christ? Shall tribulation, or distress, or persecution, or famine, or nakedness, or peril, or sword? . . . No, in all these things we are more than conquerors through him who loved us. For I am sure that neither death, nor life, nor angels, nor principalities, nor things present, nor things to come, nor powers, nor height, nor depth, nor anything else in all creation, will be able to separate us from the love of God in Christ Jesus our Lord.

—Romans 8:18–26,31,32,35,37–39

Lord,
Turn my sighs into songs.

8 *Greater Love Has No Man....*

The incidents of which we were hearing now impressed us profoundly. One that went the rounds soon after concerned another Argyll. He was in a work detail on the railroad. The day's work had ended; the tools were being counted. When the party was about to be dismissed the Japanese guard declared that a shovel was missing. He insisted someone had stolen it to sell to the Thais. He strode up and down in front of the men, ranting and denouncing them for their wickedness, their stupidity, and, most unforgivable of all, their ingratitude to the Emperor.

Screaming in broken English, he demanded that the guilty one step forward to take his punishment. No one moved. The guard's rage reached new heights of violence.

"All die! All die!" he shrieked.

To show that he meant what he said, he pulled back the bolt, put the rifle to his shoulder, and looked down the sights, ready to fire at the first man he saw at the end of them. At that moment the Argyll stepped forward, stood stiffly to attention, and said calmly, "I did it."

The guard unleashed all his whipped-up hatred; he kicked the hapless prisoner and beat him with his fists. Still the Argyll stood rigidly at attention. The blood was streaming down his face, but he made no sound. His silence goaded the guard to an excess of rage. He seized his rifle by the barrel and lifted it high over his head. With a final howl he brought the butt down on the skull of the Argyll, who sank limply to the ground and did not move. Although it was perfectly evident that he was dead, the guard continued to beat

him and stopped only when exhausted. The men of the
work detail picked up their comrade's body, shouldered
their tools, and marched back to camp. When the tools
were counted again at the guardhouse no shovel was
missing.

—Ernest Gordon, chaplain

Surely he has borne our griefs
  and carried our sorrows. . . .
But he was wounded for our transgressions,
  he was bruised for our iniquities;
upon him was the chastisement that made us whole,
  and with his stripes we are healed.
He was oppressed, and he was afflicted,
  yet he opened not his mouth;
like a lamb that is led to the slaughter,
  and like a sheep that before its shearers is dumb,
  so he opened not his mouth.

—Isaiah 53:4,5,7

This doctrine of the cross is sheer folly to those on
their way to ruin, but to us who are on the way to
salvation it is the power of God. Scripture says, "I will
destroy the wisdom of the wise, and bring to nothing
the cleverness of the clever." Where is your wise man
now, your man of learning, or your subtle debater—
limited, all of them, to this passing age? God has made
the wisdom of this world look foolish. As God in his
wisdom ordained, the world failed to find him by its
wisdom, and he chose to save those who have faith by
the folly of the Gospel. Jews call for miracles, Greeks
look for wisdom; but we proclaim Christ—yes, Christ
nailed to the cross; and though this is a stumbling-
block to Jews and folly to Greeks, yet to those who
have heard his call, Jews and Greeks alike, he is the
power of God and the wisdom of God.

Divine folly is wiser than the wisdom of man, and divine weakness stronger than man's strength. My brothers, think what sort of people you are, whom God has called. Few of you are men of wisdom, by any human standard; few are powerful or highly born. Yet, to shame the wise, God has chosen what the world counts folly, and to shame what is strong, God has chosen what the world counts weakness.

—*I Corinthians 1:18–27* (NEB)

I have been crucified with Christ: the life I now live is not my life, but the life which Christ lives in me; and my present bodily life is lived by faith in the son of God, who loved me and sacrificed himself for me.

—*Galatians 2:20* (NEB)

Lord, I remember you,
              your cross,
              your love for me,
              your sacrifice.
    I remember those persons who have sacrificed
              energy,
              ease,
              money,
              joy,
               for me.
Make me willing to spend myself
              for those whose lives are bound up
              with my own.
Lord, I remember you.

9 *Shoes and Weeds*

FATHER URBAN was a priest—manly, kind, with a sense of humor. One time he found himself on an island a few hundred yards off the shore of a private lake with an attractive woman named Sally, who liked him and who, as the sun went down, set out to seduce him. She invited him to go swimming. He refused. She said she would go anyway. In a matter of moments she was standing before him in front of the fire, her back to him, wearing nothing but her shoes. They were high-heeled shoes, golden calf.

"All right," she said, turning around. "Try and stop me." "You've got me covered," he said, and took his eyes off her, and kept them off, commending himself. It was like tearing up telephone directories, the hardest part was getting started. "*Not* going to stop me?" "No, I'll wait...."

The first shoe hit him on the shoulder, a glancing blow, and landed in the dead ashes at the front of the fire, from which he quickly retrieved it, but the second one struck him on the head.

"Hey," he yelled, but did not turn around and look at her. The second shoe had hurt. It might have killed him. What a way to go.... He stood the shoes together, and, looking at them there, felt sorry for Sally. Life here below, no matter how much you might wish it otherwise, was shoes—not champagne, but shoes, and not dirt, but shoes, and this, roughly speaking, was the mind of the Church.

—*J. F. Powers,* novelist

* * *

And this, roughly speaking, is the nature of Christian self-denial—the heroic choice of shoes over champagne or dirt, day after day, in little decisions as well as large ones—courage to choose the shoes of ultimate loyalties over the bare feet of partial commitments, the shoes of abiding joys over the slippers of quick kicks and profits. The capacity for this kind of self-denial cannot be grabbed at in a moment of temptation or trial—such moments only reveal whether you have it or not. It comes only by turning away from the smallest, most trivial wrongs with daily little wrenches of the will.

* * *

You cannot play with the animal in you without becoming wholly animal, play with falsehood without forfeiting your right to truth, play with cruelty without losing your sensitivity of mind. He who wants to keep his garden tidy doesn't reserve a plot for weeds.

—*Dag Hammarskjold,* statesman

Now Joseph was handsome and good-looking. And after a time his master's wife cast her eyes upon Joseph, and said, "Lie with me." But he refused and said to his master's wife . . . "Lo, having me my master has no concern about anything in the house, and he has put everything that he has in my hand. . . . How then can I do this great wickedness, and sin against God?" And although she spoke to Joseph day after day, he would not listen to her, to lie with her or to be with her. But one day, when he went into the house to do his work and none of the men of the house was there in the house, she caught him by his garment, saying, "Lie with me." But he left his garment in her hand, and fled and got out of the house. And when she saw that he had left his garment in her hand, and had fled

[33]

out of the house, she called to the men of her household and said to them, "See, he has brought among us a Hebrew to insult us; he came in to lie with me, and I cried out with a loud voice; and when he heard that I lifted up my voice and cried, he left his garment with me, and fled and got out of the house."

—*Genesis 39:6–15* (incomplete)

For we have not a high priest who is unable to sympathize with our weaknesses, but one who in every respect has been tempted as we are. . . . For because he himself has suffered and been tempted, he is able to help those who are tempted. . . . Let us then with confidence draw near to the throne of grace, that we may receive mercy and find grace to help in time of need.

—*Hebrews 4:15; 2:18; 4:16*

You know what I am going through, Lord.
You know how weak I am.
    Strengthen me;
    cool my desire;
    quiet me,
        and make me loyal.

Thank you, Lord.

10 *Two Lonely People*

We hurried on, our heads bent against the wind, to the cluster of lights ahead that was 149th Street and Westchester Avenue, and those lights seemed to me the brightest lights I had ever seen. Tugging at my father's coat, I started down the line of pushcarts. . . . I would merely pause before a pushcart to say, with as much control as I could muster, "Look at that chemistry set!" or, "There's a stamp album!" or, "Look at the printing press!" Each time my father would pause and ask the pushcart man the price. Then without a word we would move on to the next pushcart. Once or twice he would pick up a toy of some kind and look at it and then at me, as if to suggest this might be something I might like, but I was ten years old and a good deal beyond just a toy; my heart was set on a chemistry set or a printing press. There they were on every pushcart we stopped at, but the price was always the same and soon I looked up and saw we were nearing the end of the line. Only two or three more pushcarts remained. My father looked up, too, and I heard him jingle some coins in his pocket. In a flash I knew it all. He'd gotten together about seventy-five cents to buy me a Christmas present, and he hadn't dared say so in case there was nothing to be had for so small a sum. As I looked up at him I saw a look of despair and disappointment in his eyes that brought me closer to him than I had ever been in my life. I wanted to throw my arms around him and say, "It doesn't matter. . . . I understand. . . . This is better than a chemistry set or a printing press. . . . I love you." But instead we stood shivering beside each other for a moment—then turned away from the last two pushcarts and started silently back home. . . . I didn't even take his hand on the way home nor did he take mine. We were not on that basis. Nor did I ever tell him how close to him I felt that night—that for a little while the concrete wall between father and son had crumbled away and I knew that we were two lonely people struggling to reach each other.

—*Moss Hart,* author

But Naomi said to her two daughters-in-law, "Go, return each of you to her mother's house. May the Lord deal kindly with you, as you have dealt with the dead and with me. The Lord grant that you may find a home, each of you in the house of her husband!" Then she kissed them, and they lifted up their voices and wept. . . . And Orpah kissed her mother-in-law, but Ruth clung to her. And she said, "See, your sister-in-law has gone back to her people and to her gods; return after your sister-in-law." But Ruth said, "Entreat me not to leave you or to return from following you; for where you go I will go, and where you lodge I will lodge; your people shall be my people, and your God my God; where you die I will die, and there will I be buried. May the Lord do so to me and more also if even death parts me from you." And when Naomi saw that she was determined to go with her, she said no more.

—*Ruth 1:8,9,14–18*

Now his elder son was in the field; and as he came and drew near to the house, he heard music and dancing. And he called one of the servants and asked what this meant. And he said to him, "Your brother has come, and your father has killed the fatted calf, because he has received him safe and sound." But he was angry and refused to go in. His father came out and entreated him, but he answered his father, "Lo, these many years I have served you, and I never disobeyed your command; yet you never gave me a kid, that I might make merry with my friends. But when this son of yours came, who has devoured your living with harlots, you killed for him the fatted calf!" And he said to him, "Son, you are always with me, and all that is mine is yours. It was fitting to make merry and be glad, for this your brother was dead, and is alive; he was lost, and is found."

—Luke 15:25-32

> We struggle in separation,
>   with silent longing,
>   lonely,
>   and alone.
>
> Lord, help us to reach out to each other,
>   and say "I love you."

II *Do You Love Me?*

The joint, as Fats Waller would have said, was jumping. . . . And, during the last set, the saxophone player took off on a terrific solo. He was a kid from some insane place like Jersey City or Syracuse, but somewhere along the line he had discovered he could say it with a saxophone. He stood there, wide-legged, humping the air, filling his barrel chest, shivering in the rags of his twenty-odd years, and screaming through the horn, "Do you love me?" "Do you love me?" "Do you love me?" And again—"Do you love me?" "Do you love me?" "Do you love me?" The same phrase unbearably, endlessly, and variously repeated with all the force the kid had. . . . The question was terrible and real. The boy was blowing with his lungs and guts out of his own short past; and somewhere in the past, in gutters or gang fights . . . in the acrid room, behind marijuana or the needles, under the smell in the precinct basement, he had received a blow from which he would never recover, and this no one wanted to believe. Do you love me? Do you love me? Do you love me? The men on the stand stayed with him cool and at a little distance, adding and questioning. . . . But each man knew that the boy was blowing for every one of them. . . .

—*James Baldwin,* author

After breakfast, Jesus said to Simon Peter,
"Simon son of John, do you love me more than all else?"
"Yes, Lord," he answered, "you know that I love you."
"Then feed my lambs," he said.

A second time he asked, "Simon son of John, do you
    love me?"
"Yes, Lord, you know I love you."
"Then tend my sheep."
A third time he said, "Simon son of John, do you
    love me?"
Peter was hurt that he asked him a third time,
"Do you love me?"
"Lord," he said, "you know everything; you know I
    love you."
Jesus said, "Feed my sheep."

—John 21:15-17 (NEB)

> Comfort, comfort my people
>   says your God.
> Speak tenderly to Jerusalem,
>   and cry to her
> That her warfare is ended,
> That her iniquity is pardoned,
> That she has received from the Lord's hand
>   double for all her sins. . . .
> Behold the Lord God comes with might,
>   and his recompense before him.
> He will feed his flock like a shepherd,
>   he will gather the lambs in his arms,
> He will carry them in his bosom,
>   and gently lead those that are with young.
>
>
>
> *—Isaiah 40:1,2,10-11*
>
>

Do you love me?
You have let me suffer,
        and let me cause others to suffer.
You have watched me get broken,
        and go sour.

You have pounded me for my sins,
and made me hard.

Lord, I know you love me
and all of us.
Speak tenderly to us
Comfort me.

12 *The Little-Ease and the Spitting Cell*

I had to submit and admit my guilt. I had to live in the little-ease. To be sure, you are not familiar with that dungeon cell that was called the little-ease in the Middle Ages. In general, one was forgotten there for life. That cell was distinguished from others by ingenious dimensions. It was not high enough to stand up in nor yet wide enough to lie down in. One had to take on an awkward manner and live on the diagonal; sleep was a collapse, and walking a squatting. *Mon cher,* there was genius—and I am weighing my words—in that so simple invention. Every day through the unchanging restriction that stiffened his body, the condemned man learned that he was guilty and that innocence consists in stretching joyously. Can you imagine in that cell a frequenter of summits and upper decks? What? One could live in those cells and still be innocent? Improbable! Highly improbable! Or else my reasoning would collapse. That innocence should be reduced to living hunchbacked—I refuse to entertain for a second such a hypothesis. Moreover, we cannot assert the innocence of anyone, whereas we can state with certainty the guilt of all. . . .

Believe me, religions are on the wrong track the moment they moralize and fulminate commandments. God is not needed to create guilt or to punish. Our fellow men suffice, aided by ourselves. You were speaking of the Last Judgment. . . . I shall wait for it resolutely, for I have known what is worse, the judgment of men. For them, no extenuating circumstances; even the good intention is ascribed to crime. Have you at least heard of the spitting cell, which a nation recently thought up to prove itself the greatest on earth? A walled-up box in which the prisoner can stand without moving. The solid door that locks him in his cement shell stops at chin level. Hence only his face is visible, and every passing jailer spits copiously on it. The prisoner, wedged into his cell, cannot wipe his face, though he is allowed, it is true, to close his eyes. Well, that, *mon cher,* is a human invention. They didn't need God for that little masterpiece.

What of it? Well, God's sole usefulness would be to guarantee innocence, and I am inclined to see religion rather as a huge laundering venture—as it was once but briefly, for exactly three years, and it wasn't called religion. Since then, soap has been lacking, our faces are dirty, and we wipe one another's noses. All dunces, all punished, let's all spit on one another and—hurry! to the little-ease! Each tries to spit first, that's all. I'll tell you a big secret, *mon cher.* Don't wait for the Last Judgment. It takes place every day.

—*Albert Camus,* author

You therefore have no defence—you who sit in judgement, whoever you may be—for in judging your fellow-man you condemn yourself, since you, the judge, are equally guilty. . . . For all alike have sinned, and are deprived of the divine splendour, and all are justified by God's free grace alone, through his act of liberation in the person of Christ Jesus.

—*Romans 2:1;3:23,24* (NEB)

And while he was proclaiming the message to them, a man was brought who was paralysed. Four men were carrying him, but because of the crowd they could not get him near. So they opened up the roof over the place where Jesus was, and when they had broken through they lowered the stretcher on which the paralysed man was lying. When Jesus saw thei.

faith, he said to the paralysed man, "My son, your sins are forgiven."

Now there were some lawyers sitting there and they thought to themselves, "Why does the fellow talk like that? This is blasphemy! Who but God alone can forgive sins?" Jesus knew in his own mind that this was what they were thinking, and said to them: "Why do you harbour thoughts like these? Is it easier to say to this paralysed man, 'Your sins are forgiven,' or to say, 'Stand up, take your bed, and walk'? But to convince you that the Son of Man has the right on earth to forgive sins"—he turned to the paralysed man—"I say to you, stand up, take your bed, and go home." And he got up, took his stretcher at once, and went out in full view of them all, so that they were astounded and praised God.

—Mark 2:3–12 (NEB)

Come to me, all who labor and are heavy laden, and I will give you rest. Take my yoke upon you, and learn from me; for I am gentle and lowly in heart, and you will find rest for your souls. For my yoke is easy, and my burden is light.

—Matthew 11:28–30

Lord, you know the little-ease in which I crouch every day.
 You know my longing to stretch joyously
  in the freedom of innocence.

Forgive my sins.
Take away the burden of my guilt.

Put your easy yoke on me,
 and I will stand up and walk again!

I3 *The Face of My Secret Heart*

Where do New Yorkers get these faces that they wear in the streets of Manhattan? . . .

One of the most interesting places to watch faces is Times Square. Times Square faces tend, on the whole, to be slightly desperate. In the early evening there are the young taut faces bent on picking up the illusory trail of pleasure. The happy imbecile faces grinning at the neon arcades. The faces of life's losers studying the lewd movie posters. The strained hungry faces of the boys who think that tonight, this night, something exciting may happen at last.

And there are the tourists' faces—harried, bland, intoxicated faces, in-from-Scarsdale faces, faces struggling to look like tough sophisticated New York faces, tired faces, betrayed faces. These Times Square faces are most all, in their way, sad. The place is a microcosm of human aimlessness, and in the early morning hours, when the mob has thinned, there are the drifting, frustrated faces of the sleepless, resigned to tomorrow's hangover.

For an antidote there is the East Side, lair of the successful face. . . . They are faces that transmit vital, tantalizing messages. "I am off to merge Consolidated," they say, without moving a jaw muscle. Or, "My prima ballerina has already been waiting 45 minutes."

For famous faces, Fifth Avenue is unbeatable. "Look," these Fifth Avenue faces say, "I am famous, and it's a great bore being looked at all the time, but see how unruffled I am by your stare. . . ."

There are more—the Village faces (Ohio faces wearing beards), Mets-fan faces (lippy, sad), Yankee-fan faces (smug), Mafia faces, Harlem faces, theater faces, faces running on Benzedrine and faces unsafe to walk with on a lonely street. . . . People are walking the streets with the most startling confessions written from chin to hairline.

—Russell Baker, journalist

Behold, thou desirest truth in the inward being;
   therefore teach me wisdom in my secret heart.
Purge me with hyssop, and I shall be clean;
   wash me, and I shall be whiter than snow.
Fill me with joy and gladness;
   let the bones which thou hast broken rejoice.
Hide thy face from my sins,
   and blot out all my iniquities.
Create in me a clean heart, O God,
   and put a new and right spirit within me. . . .
a broken and contrite heart, O God,
    thou wilt not despise.

—Psalm 51:6–10,17b

I sought the Lord, and he answered me,
    and delivered me from all my fears.
Look to him, and be radiant;
    so your faces shall never be ashamed.
This poor man cried, and the Lord heard him,
    and saved him out of all his troubles.

—Psalm 34:4–6

Since we have such a hope, we are very bold, and not like Moses, who put a veil over his face. . . . But when a man turns to the Lord, the veil is removed. Now the Lord is the Spirit, and where the Spirit of the Lord is, there is freedom. And we all, with unveiled face, beholding the glory of the Lord, are being changed into his likeness from one degree of glory to another. . . . For it is the God who said, "Let light shine out of darkness," who has shone in our hearts to give the light of the knowledge of the glory of God in the face of Christ.

—*II Corinthians 3:12,13a,16–18a; 4:6*

O God, heal my heart
and forgive my face.

MURRAY, in his thirties, rebels against conventional society and, temporarily unemployed, has care of his twelve-year-old nephew. A social worker comes to discuss taking the boy out of Murray's charge on grounds that he is an unfit guardian. Murray expresses his concern for the boy's future.

And he started to make *lists* this year. Lists of everything; subway stops, underwear, what he's gonna do next week. If somebody doesn't watch out he'll start making lists of what he's gonna do the next ten years. Hey, suppose they put him in with a whole family of list-makers? He'll learn to know everything before it happens, he'll learn how to be one of the nice dead people. . . . I just want him to stay with me till I can be sure he won't turn into *Norman Nothing*. I want to be sure he'll know when he's chickening out on himself. I want him to get to know exactly the special thing he is or else he won't notice it when it starts to go. I want him to stay awake and know who the phonies are. I want him to know how to holler and put up an argument, I want a little guts to show before I can let him go. I want to be sure he sees all the wild possibilities. I want him to know it's worth all the trouble just to give the world a little goosing when you get the chance. And I want him to know the subtle, sneaky, important reason why he was born a human being and not a chair. I will be very sorry to see him go. The kid was the best straight man I ever had. He is a laugher, and laughers are rare. I mean, you tell that kid something funny—not just any piece of corn, but something funny, and he'll give you your money's worth. It's not just funny jokes he reads, or

I tell him, that he laughs at. Not just set-up funny stuff. He sees street jokes, he has the good eye, he sees subway farce and cross town bus humor and all the cartoons people make by being alive. He has a good eye. And I don't want him to leave until I'm certain he'll never be ashamed of it.

—*Herb Gardner,* playwright

Woe to you, scribes and Pharisees, hypocrites! for you tithe mint and dill and cummin, and have neglected the weightier matters of the law, justice and mercy and faith; these you ought to have done, without neglecting the others. You blind guides, straining out a gnat and swallowing a camel!

Woe to you, scribes and Pharisees, hypocrites! for you cleanse the outside of the cup and of the plate, but inside they are full of extortion and rapacity. You blind Pharisee! first cleanse the inside of the cup and of the plate, that the outside also may be clean.

Woe to you, scribes and Pharisees, hypocrites! for you are like whitewashed tombs, which outwardly appear beautiful, but within they are full of dead men's bones and all uncleanness. So you also outwardly appear righteous to men, but within you are full of hypocrisy and iniquity.

—*Matthew 23:23–28*

Christ set us free, to be free men. . . .

You, my friends, were called to be free men; only do not turn your freedom into licence for your lower nature, but be servants to one another in love. For the whole law can be summed up in a single commandment: "Love your neighbour as yourself!" But if you go on fighting one another, tooth and nail, all you can expect is mutual destruction. I mean this: if you are guided by the Spirit you will not fulfill the desires of your lower nature. That nature sets its desires against the Spirit, while the Spirit fights against it. They are in conflict with one another so that what you will to do you cannot do. But if you are led by the Spirit, you are not under law. Anyone can see the kind of behaviour that belongs to the lower nature; fornication, impurity, and indecency; idolatry and sorcery; quarrels, a contentious temper, envy, fits of rage, selfish ambitions, and the like. I warn you, as I warned you before, that those who behave in such ways will never inherit the kingdom of God. But the harvest of the Spirit is love, joy, peace, patience, kindness, goodness, fidelity, gentleness, and self-control. There is no law dealing with such things as these. And those who belong to Christ Jesus have crucified the lower nature with its passions and desires. If the Spirit is the source of our life, let the Spirit also direct our course.

—Galatians 5:1,13–25 (NEB)

You have set me free, Lord!
　Free from fingers shaking at me,
　　　　from voices saying "naughty, naughty,"
　　　　from fear of my own unique being.

You have set me free, Lord!
　Free to choose another's good over my own,
　　　　to go the second mile,
　　　　to turn the other cheek.

You have set me free, Lord!
　Free to take others quite seriously,
　free from taking myself too seriously.
Let me laugh while I make up my lists!

I 5 _So Willing to Give_

We all knew the danger was increasing. Threats came daily, cruel and cold and constant, against us and the children. But we had lived with this hatred for years and we did not let it corrode us.

In a funny way, the constant threat of death made life richer and more meaningful—it made us more aware of each other, and it brought us closer together. When he left in the morning, I never knew if I would see him again. We never parted in anger, because we couldn't afford to.

As soon as Medgar took the NAACP job, the threats began. During crisis times the phone would ring all night. At first I tried to talk to the callers, but that was hopeless. Then I started hanging up, but they just called right back. Finally—and I've done this for years now—I began putting the phone quietly down on the table and letting them talk to the empty wall. So much hatred has been poured on that wall!

At home, we learned to stay away from the windows at night lest we become a target. Recently he had taught the children to fall to the floor, infantry fashion, if they heard a sharp noise outside.

Until recently Medgar wasn't really worried. All over the state he worked furiously on the two approaches he always believed are keys to the southern Negro's future. The first is the ballot box, the second is economic boycott. "If we can get rid of our sense of inferiority," he always said, "we can begin to win our equality peacefully." This conviction that the Negro is not inferior—this was the thing, above all else, that he was trying to get across.

When the last series of demonstrations began in

jackson, the other side seemed to realize the serious-ness, too. The threats against all of us intensified. Then about a month ago the first attack on our home came in the form of a fire bomb.

It bathed the carport in flames. I was afraid someone was waiting outside to shoot us, but as the flames billowed up I forgot my fear and ran out to douse them with a garden hose.

Perhaps this incident began to prey on Medgar's mind. By the week before he was killed, he was nearly exhausted. He had been working 20 hours a day for months. I think that on that last Sunday we spent together he knew something was going to happen.

On Monday he was very busy. He mentioned death again that day, I remember, and again on Tuesday morning before he left. He kissed each of the children that morning, and he held me in his arms a long time.

He called three times from his office that day. I laughed and asked how he found time, and he said he wanted to hear my voice. The last thing he told me was that he loved me and he loved the children. "I'll see you tonight," he said.

For some reason I let the children stay up all hours that night. We heard the car stop and the door open and then we heard the shot. I knew instantly that Medgar had been shot.

When I jerked open the front door, he had staggered from the car to the steps with his keys in his hand, trying to come home. He fell face downward and there was blood everywhere—everywhere. I fell on my knees and lifted his head. He seemed to be struggling, perhaps to speak or perhaps to live. Then they took him to the hospital.

The next day when the police and other white people came, I looked out and saw them and, for a moment, I hated everybody with a white skin. But that didn't last. Medgar had taught me not to hate and today I feel no hate for anyone, not even the man who killed him.

I have magnificent memories. Medgar didn't belong just to me—he belonged to so many, many people everywhere. He was so willing to give his life that I feel his death has served a certain purpose.

—*Myrlie Evers,* housewife

By the waters of Babylon,
    there we sat down and wept,
    when we remembered Zion.
On the willows there
    we hung up our lyres,
For there our captors
    required of us songs. . . .
How shall we sing the Lord's song
    in a foreign land? . . .

O daughter of Babylon, you devastator!
    Happy shall he be who requites you
    with what you have done to us!
Happy shall he be who takes your little ones
    and dashes them against the rock!

—*Psalm 137:1–3a,4,8,9*

Need I say more? Time is too short for me to tell the stories of Gideon, Barak, Samson, and Jephthah, of David and Samuel and the prophets. Through faith they overthrew kingdoms, established justice, saw God's promises fulfilled. They muzzled ravening lions, quenched the fury of fire, escaped death by the sword. Their weakness was turned to strength. . . . Women received back their dead raised to life. Others were tortured to death, disdaining release, to win a better resurrection. Others, again, had to face jeers and flogging, even fetters and prison bars. They were stoned, they were sawn in two, they were put to the sword . . . they went about . . . in poverty, distress, and misery. They were too good for this world. . . .

And what of ourselves? With all these witnesses to faith around us like a cloud, we must throw off every encumbrance, every sin to which we cling, and run with resolution the race for which we are entered, our eyes fixed on Jesus . . . who, for the sake of the joy that lay ahead of him, endured the cross. . . .
—*Hebrews 11:32–12:2* (NEB) (incomplete)

Amen! Amen!

16 O.K., I'm Scared

I remember the first day that I visited Germantown Friends School. I wandered through very big halls, carrying very big books, among very big people. And I was so afraid that when the guys at my lunch table told me that it was ancient G.F.S. tradition for the new students to clean up the lunch room, I wholeheartedly believed them.

But William Faulkner wrote: "The basis of all things is to be afraid." I hope this is true. At least it is comforting.

We begin school, we begin to make friends. We forget to invite someone to a party, or they forget to invite us. We deny someone an easy "hello" on a blue morning. We receive or inflict what seems like very great hurt and is probably, most of the time, completely unintentional. We move from the unselfish openness of children. What we expect never comes or comes at the wrong time or in the wrong wrappings. So we, or at least I, protect the self by concentrating on homework or guitar or football, or by becoming hard and powerful, or by saying, "I don't care." However slightly, we make ourselves less vulnerable. Perhaps, as we grow older, the hurts only seem to increase because our defenses are failing. In any case, our fears are justified.

And at the same time that we are a little wary, a bit critical of others, we are afraid of being alone. We want to be a part of something or someone. There are enough committees, enough athletic teams to go around. But we compete destructively for successful grades, for influential friends, for the confidence that is brought by the external recognition of some sort of talent. And even our talents are frightening because they demand a devotion that limits and isolates us, an openness or creativity that has already proved painful.

Then every now and then we are hit by a greater fear, beyond ourselves and our relations with others. We read the Bible or the newspaper and realize, in spite of intelligence, in spite of education, how overwhelming is the nature of man, how impossible the goals of truth and love.

"The basis of all things is to be afraid." But perhaps we can learn to accept being afraid, accept reservation as part of our relations with others, accept the uneasiness of being alone and the fear of miscalculating our capabilities.

If we could only say, "I'm scared. O.K., I should be scared," and then take a chance, make up a song and sing it to others, all the while not knowing whether the notes are right for our voice or whether anyone will want to listen. And if we could only sing our song, not to drown out others, not expecting them to sing along, but with the hope that they will create and sing one, too, so that we can listen.

—*Thomas R. Large,* high school senior

My son, if you receive my words
and treasure up my commandments
  with you,
making your ear attentive to
  wisdom
and inclining your heart to
  understanding;
Yes, if you cry out for insight
  and raise your voice for understanding,
if you seek it like silver
  and search for it as for hidden treasures;

then you will understand the fear
of the Lord
and find the knowledge of God.

—*Proverbs 2:1–5*

For all who are moved by the Spirit of God are sons
of God. The Spirit you have received is not a spirit
of slavery leading you back into a life of fear, but a
Spirit that makes us sons, enabling us to cry "Abba!
Father!" In that cry the Spirit of God joins with our
spirit in testifying that we are God's children; and if
children, then heirs. We are God's heirs and Christ's
fellow-heirs, if we share his sufferings now in order
to share his spendour hereafter.

—*Romans 8:14–17* (NEB)

My heart is ready, O God,
my heart is ready!
I will sing, I will sing praises!
Awake, my soul!
Awake, O harp and lyre!
I will awake the dawn!

—*Psalm 108:1, 2*

O.K., I'm scared. I admit it.
Scared of the lust and deceit and jealousy
biding their time in me,
waiting for a weak moment . . .
scared of the possibility that I don't have
the stuff to succeed in the terms I've set for myself . . .
scared that I might fail, might be failing now,
with my children, in my marriage, with my
friends . . .
scared that I may have missed the boat already . . .
and not be aware of it.

I'm scared because I've forgotten who I am.
  I am your son, Lord,
  heir to all that you would give me.

I'm scared because I've forgotten who you are.
  You are my father, Lord;
  your Spirit is moving me with power.

I will not be afraid, for you are with me.

17 *Separation, Longing, and Prayer*

In my experience nothing tortures us so much as longing. . . . When we are forcibly separated from those we love, we simply cannot, like so many others, contrive for ourselves some cheap substitute elsewhere —I don't mean because of moral considerations, but because we are what we are. . . . All we can do is to wait patiently; we must suffer the unutterable agony of separation, and feel the longing until it makes us sick. For that is the only way in which we can preserve our relationship with our loved ones unimpaired. There have been a few occasions in my life when I have had to learn what homesickness means. There is no agony worse than this, and during these months in prison I have sometimes been terribly homesick. And as I am sure you will have to go through the same agony during these coming months, I wanted to tell what I had learnt from it in case it may be of some help to you. The first and invariable effect of such longing is an itching desire to abandon the daily routine, with the result that our lives become disordered. I used to be tempted to stay in bed after six in the morning . . . and to sleep on. Up to now I have never succumbed to that temptation. I realized that that would have been the first stage of capitulation, and no doubt worse would have followed. . . . Another point, I am sure it is best not to talk to strangers about our feelings; that only makes matters worse, though we should always be ready to listen to the troubles of others. Above all, we must never give way to self-pity. . . .

We must simply hold out and win through. That sounds very hard at first, but at the same time it is a great consolation, since leaving the gap unfilled preserves the bonds between us. It is nonsense to say that God fills the gap; he does not fill it, but keeps it empty so that our communion with another may be kept alive, even at the cost of pain. . . . The dearer and richer our memories, the more difficult the separation. But gratitude converts the pangs of memory into a tranquil joy. The beauties of the past are not endured as a thorn in the flesh, but as a gift precious for its sake. We must not wallow in our memories or surrender to them, just as we don't gaze all the time at a valuable present, but get it out from time to time, and for the rest hide it away as a treasure we know is there all the time. . . . It has been borne in upon me here with peculiar force that a concrete situation can always be mastered, and that only fear and anxiety magnify them to an immeasurable degree beforehand. From the moment we awake until we fall asleep we must commend our loved ones wholly and unreservedly to God, and leave them in his hands, transforming our anxiety for them into prayers on their behalf.

—*Dietrich Bonhoeffer,* theologian

I thank my God in all my remembrance of you, always in every prayer of mine for you all making my prayer with joy, thankful for your partnership in the gospel from the first day until now. And I am sure that he who began a good work in you will bring it to completion at the day of Jesus Christ. It is right for me to feel thus about you all, because I hold you in my heart, for you are all partakers with me of grace, both in my imprisonment and in the defense and confirmation of the gospel. For God is my witness, how I yearn for you all with the affection of Christ Jesus. And it is my prayer that your love may abound more and more, with knowledge and all discernment, so that you may approve what is excellent, and may be pure and blameless for the day of Christ, filled with the fruits of righteousness which come through Jesus Christ, to the glory and praise of God. I want you to know, brethren, that what has happened to me has really served to advance the gospel, so that it has become known throughout the whole praetorian guard and to all the rest that my imprisonment is for Christ; and most of the brethren have been made confident in the Lord because of my imprisonment, and are much more bold to speak the word of God without fear.

—Philippians 1:3-14

For thus says the Lord God: Behold I, I myself will search for my sheep, and will seek them out. As a shepherd seeks out his flock when some of his sheep have been scattered abroad, so will I seek out my sheep; and I will rescue them from all places where they have been scattered on a day of clouds and thick darkness. And I will bring them out from the peoples, and gather them from the countries, and will bring them into their own land; and I will feed them on the mountains of Israel, by the fountains, and in all the inhabited places of the country. I will feed them with good pasture, and upon the mountain heights of Israel shall be their pasture; there they shall lie down in good grazing land, and on fat pasture they shall feed on the mountains of Israel. I myself will be the shepherd of my sheep, and I will make them lie down, says the Lord God. I will seek the lost, and I will bring back the strayed, and I will bind up the crippled, and I will strengthen the weak, and the fat and the strong I will watch over; I will feed them in justice.

—Ezekiel 34:11-16

Therefore, my brethren, whom I love and long for, my joy and crown, stand firm thus in the Lord, my beloved. . . . Rejoice in the Lord always; again I will say rejoice. Let all men know your forebearance. The Lord is at hand. Have no anxiety about anything, but in everything by prayer and supplication with thanksgiving let your requests be made known to God. And the peace of God, which passes all understanding, will keep your hearts and your minds in Christ Jesus.

—Philippians 4:1, 4-7

O God, in your presence I think of those
    from whom I am separated by distance,
        misunderstanding,
        circumstance,
        death.

You know the ache of my longing for————.
Strengthen me to hold out and win through.
Grant me faith to entrust those I love
    to your care,
with the confidence of Bonhoeffer
and the joy of Paul.

Thank you, Lord.

I 8 *Not Built for Comfort*

A conscience is not a gadget built for comfort, but an internal time bomb. It ticks away the days, ready at a decisive moment to blow your life apart by turning you against your self-interest or setting you apart from your neighbors.

Ask a man who knows. Until recently, Jack Shea, Jr., 41, was a successful, high-pay oil executive in Dallas. As the senior vice-president and a director of American Petrofina Company of Texas, he bossed Fina's refinery operations and gas and oil sales throughout its market. . . . The company's annual reports paid tribute to his work as the key to its fast growth in a competitive industry. Shea would become Fina's chief executive in a year or so, insiders thought, and the dedicated men under him were ready to roll. . . .

Then . . . came the assassination of President Kennedy.

Jack Shea, like many Americans, found in the national tragedy a call to deeper dedication. . . . He berated himself for having been so wrapped up in business that he failed to be much of a citizen. He had stood silent, with most Dallas moderates, while the city became the victim of fanatic minorities. . . . Shea knew that it was time for somebody in Dallas to face the situation honestly, whatever the risk. . . . You may remember his "Memo About a Dallas Citizen" (*Look,* March 24, 1964). . . .

Jack Shea had to quit his job. . . . How did it happen? . . . "About a month after the article, and hours after the Dallas *Morning News* took me to its editorial-page woodshed a second time, I was suddenly confronted with a company demand: I must agree never to comment publicly without formally clearing each word in advance and in writing. The issue was not *what* I said, but whether I could say anything at all. . . . The company demand made it simple for me. I suggested we might as well discuss my resignation. . . . You don't sign away your citizenship for pay. The company policy reached beyond business into personal belief. I would have been promising never to exercise the right and responsibility of a citizen."

Jack Shea quietly burned a hole into the Dallas conscience. . . . His Saturday golf foursome at Brook Hollow found another fourth. His name vanished from his locker door. . . . On a rare visit to the club, old "friends" cut him cold. . . . One oilman boasted sure knowledge that "Shea was on the skids at Fina and had nothing to lose anyway. . . ." Conscience has to be explained away.

—T George Harris

He showed me: behold, the Lord was standing beside a wall built with a plumb line, with a plumb line in his hand. And the Lord said to me, "Amos, what do you see?" And I said, "A plumb line." Then the Lord said, "Behold I am setting a plumb line
    in the midst of my people Israel;
    I will never again pass by them;
    the high places of Isaac shall be made desolate,
    and the sanctuaries of Israel shall be laid waste,
    and I will rise against the house of Jeroboam
      with the sword."
Then Amaziah the priest of Bethel sent to Jeroboam king of Israel, saying, "Amos has conspired against you in the midst of the house of Israel; the land is not able to bear all his words. For thus Amos has said, 'Jeroboam shall die by the sword,

and Israel must go into exile
away from his land.' "
And Amaziah said to Amos, "O Seer, go, flee away
to the land of Judah, and eat bread there, and
prophesy there; but never again prophesy at
Bethel, for it is the king's sanctuary, and it is
a temple of the kingdom."
Then Amos answered Amaziah, "I am no prophet, nor
a prophet's son, but I am a herdsman, and a dresser
of sycamore trees, and the Lord took me from
following the flock, and the Lord said to me, 'Go,
prophesy to my people Israel.'

Now therefore hear the word of the Lord.
You say, 'Do not prophesy against Israel,
        and do not preach against the house of Isaac.'
Therefore thus says the Lord:
        'Your wife shall be a harlot in the city,
            and your sons and your daughters shall fall
                by the sword,
            and your land shall be parceled out by line;
You yourself shall die in an unclean land,
            and Israel shall surely go into exile away
                from its land.' "

—Amos 7:7–17

Now about that time, the Christian movement gave
rise to a serious disturbance. There was a man named
Demetrius, a silver-smith who made silver shrines
of Diana and provided a great deal of employment
for the craftsmen. He called a meeting of these men
and the workers in allied trades, and addressed them.
"Men," he said, "you know that our high standard
of living depends on this industry. And you see and
hear how this fellow Paul with his propaganda has
perverted crowds of people, not only at Ephesus
but also in practically the whole province of Asia.

He is telling them that gods made by human hands are not gods at all. There is danger for us here; it is not only that our line of business will be discredited, but also that the sanctuary of the great goddess Diana will cease to command respect. . . ." When they heard this they were roused to fury and shouted, "Great is Diana of the Ephesians!" The whole city was in confusion. . . .

—Acts 19:23–28 (NEB)

So they ordered them to leave the court, and then discussed the matter among themselves. "What are we going to do with these men?" they said; "for it is common knowledge in Jerusalem that a notable miracle has come about through them; and we cannot deny it. But to stop this from spreading further among the people, we had better caution them never again to speak to anyone in this name." They then called them in and ordered them to refrain from all public speaking and teaching in the name of Jesus. But Peter and John said in reply: "Is it right in God's eyes for us to obey you rather than God? Judge for yourselves. We cannot possibly give up speaking of things we have seen and heard."

—Acts 4:15–20 (NEB)

Lord, give me the courage of my convictions.
Make me put up or shut up.

19 *I Realize How Much I Was Gypped*

The lips are curved into an obliging, fixed half-smile. The grey hair is coiffured with mathematical precision, cleft exactly by the part. At the neck, not entirely masked by the photographer's shadows, a few age lines can be discerned. . . . Simone de Beauvoir has no husband and no children; by design, she has denied herself the rewards, or the burdens, of maternity. The smile is unreal, put on, perhaps, for the photographer; she cannot accept or endure the fact that she is now 57. Her mortality has obsessed her for a generation.

"Since 1944, the most important, the most irreparable thing that has happened to me is that I have grown old. How is it that time, which has no form or substance, can crush me with so huge a weight that I can no longer breathe? . . ."

She was the Mother Hubbard of existentialism, a clock in a refrigerator, a cerebral Joan of Arc. . . . Simone de Beauvoir attained everything that she ever aspired to as a girl; celebrity as a writer, the full exercise of her rebel spirit. Nevertheless, at 57, she finds herself—

". . . . hostile to the society to which I belonged, banished by my age from the future, stripped fiber by fiber from my past. If it had at least enriched the earth," she writes, summing up her life. "If it had given birth to . . . what? A hill? A rocket? The promises have all been kept. And yet, turning an incredulous gaze toward that young and credulous girl, I realize with stupor how much I was gypped."

—*Time* article on Simone de Beauvoir

Vanity of vanities, says the Preacher,
    vanity of vanities! All is vanity. . . .
All things are full of weariness;
    a man cannot utter it;
The eye is not satisfied with seeing,
    nor the ear filled with hearing.
What has been is what will be,
    and what has been done is what will be done;
    and there is nothing new under the sun. . . .
It is an unhappy business that God has given to
    the sons of men to be busy with. I have seen
    everything that is done under the sun; and behold,
All is vanity and a striving after wind. . . .
For of the wise man as of the fool there is no
    enduring remembrance, seeing that in the days to
    come all will have been long forgotten. How the wise
    man dies just like the fool! So I hated life. . . .
                    —*Ecclesiastes 1:2,8,9,13,14; 2:16,17*

As a father pities his children,
    so the Lord pities those who fear him.
For he knows our frame;
    he remembers that we are dust.
As for man, his days are like grass;
    he flourishes like a flower of the field;
for the wind passes over it, and it is gone,
    and its place knows it no more.
But the steadfast love of the Lord is from
    everlasting to everlasting
    upon those who fear him. . . .
                    —*Psalm 103:13–17a*

How blest are those who know that they are poor;
    the kingdom of Heaven is theirs.
How blest are the sorrowful;
    they shall find consolation.

How blest are those of a gentle spirit;
  they shall have the earth for their possession.
How blest are those who hunger and thirst to see
    right prevail;
  they shall be satisfied.
How blest are those who show mercy;
  mercy shall be shown to them.
How blest are those whose hearts are pure;
  they shall see God.
How blest are the peace makers;
  God shall call them his sons.
How blest are those who have suffered persecution
    for the cause of right;
  the kingdom of Heaven is theirs.
                    —*Matthew 5:3–10* (NEB)

Lord, deliver me from self-pity
        and the hatred of my life.

Keep me from gypping myself and those closest to me
      out of the joy of living.

Take me into the problems and hopes of others,
      to give and find your blessing.

20 *The Courage to Cut*

Did Panaït Petre ever tell you about a forester he met soon after he joined the Party? Long wooden shoots had been built in the forest to slide tree-trunks down the slope to the valley and into the river. They were hundreds of yards long, smooth and polished inside, and the foresters used them as well. They'd sit on the floor of the shoot, or an axe-handle, and go tobogganing down to save themselves the trouble of walking. Well, this man caught his foot in a hole in the shoot and couldn't get it free, and at that moment he heard a shout of warning, which meant that a trunk was on its way down. He saw the thing coming, and as he still couldn't free his foot he hacked it off with an axe and jumped clear just in time. He was crippled for life, but at least he was alive.

—Petru Dumitriu, novelist

If your right eye leads you astray, tear it out and fling it away; it is better for you to lose one part of your body than for the whole of it to be thrown into hell. And if your right hand is your undoing, cut it off and fling it away; it is better for you to lose one part of your body than for the whole of it to go to hell.

—Matthew 5:29,30

For the wound of the daughter of my people is my heart wounded,
    I mourn, and dismay has taken hold on me.
Is there no balm in Gilead?
    Is there no physician there?

Why then has the health of the daughter of my people
not been restored?

—Jeremiah 8:21-22

> I will heal their faithlessness:
>> I will love them freely,
>> for my anger has turned from them.

—Hosea 14:4

O God, give me courage to cut out of my life
    that liaison which is threatening
        my family's happiness,
    that indulgence which is sapping
        my strength of purpose,
    that doubt which is leading
        me to disobey you,
    that disobedience which is causing
        me to doubt you.

Heal my faithlessness,
    and restore me to health

Dear Folks,

Thank you for everything, but I am going to Chicago and try and start some kind of new life.

You asked me why I did those things and why I gave you so much trouble, and the answer is easy for me to give you, but I am wondering if you will understand.

Remember when I was about six or seven and I used to want you to just listen to me? I remember all the nice things you gave me for Christmas and my birthday and I was really happy with the things—about a week—at the time I got the things, but the rest of the time during the year I really didn't want presents, I just wanted all the time for you to listen to me like I was somebody who felt things too, because I remember even when I was young I felt things. But you said you were busy.

Mom, you are a wonderful cook, and you had everything so clean and you were tired so much from doing all those things that made you busy; but, you know something, Mom? I would have liked crackers and peanut butter just as well if you had only sat down with me a while during the day and said to me: "Tell me all about it so I can maybe help you understand!"

And when Donna came I couldn't understand why everyone made so much fuss because I didn't think it was my fault that her hair is curly and her skin so white, and she doesn't have to wear glasses with such thick lenses. Her grades were better too, weren't they?

If Donna ever has children, I hope you will tell her

to just pay some attention to the one who doesn't smile very much because that one will really be crying inside. And when she's about to bake six dozen cookies, to make sure first, that the kids don't want to tell her about a dream or a hope or something, because thoughts are important too, to small kids even though they don't have so many words to use when they tell about what they have inside them.

I think that all the kids who are doing so many things that grown-ups are tearing out their hair worrying about are really looking for somebody that will have time to listen a few minutes and who really and truly will treat them as they would a grown-up who might be useful to them, you know—polite to them. If you folks had ever said to me: "Pardon me" when you interrupted me, I'd have dropped dead!

If anybody asks you where I am, tell them I've gone looking for somebody with time because I've got a lot of things I want to talk about.

Love to all,
Your Son
—A boy with a record as a
juvenile delinquent

"Cast me not off, forsake me not,
O God of my salvation!
For my father and my mother have forsaken me,
but the Lord will take me up."
—*Psalm 27:9,10*

While they were on their way Jesus came to a village where a woman named Martha made him welcome in her home. She had a sister, Mary, who seated herself at the Lord's feet and stayed there listening to his words. Now Martha was distracted by her many tasks, so she came to him and said, "Lord, do you not care that my sister has left me to get on with the work by myself? Tell her to come and lend a hand." But the Lord answered, "Martha, Martha, you are fretting and fussing about so many things; but one thing is necessary. The part that Mary has chosen is best. . . ."

—Luke 10:38–42a (NEB)

They even brought babies for him to touch; but when the disciples saw them, they scolded them for it. But Jesus called for the children and said, "Let the little ones come to me; do not try to stop them; for the kingdom of God belongs to such as these. I tell you that whoever does not accept the kingdom of God like a child will never enter it."

—Luke 18:15–17 (NEB)

Lord, forgive me!
Forgive me for being too busy
    to realize that my wife has feelings too;
        too busy
    to let my child interrupt me while I
      read the paper or watch TV;
        too busy
    to try to understand the complaints
      of my associates at work.

Help me today, while there is still time,
    to listen.

22 *What's Your Disguise?*

There is nothing quite like the shame that a proud and sensitive man feels when, in front of thousands of admirers and surrounded by cameras and critics, he is physically demolished by another man, Floyd Patterson was saying at his camp today.

It produces a despair far deeper than anything experienced by men who might fail, say, as actors, writers, business executives or politicians. These other men, when they fail, may do so in private, he said, or they may attribute their defeats to other people. But the fighter fails alone, loses everything under the glaring lights of a public arena. "And then," Patterson said, "the fighter must climb through the ring, walk down the aisle, and face those people. This is the worst part about losing," he said, "facing the people." And it is one reason why he carries an attaché case filled with disguises into his dressing room before each fight. It will enable him to make a quick exit unrecognized, should he lose. Each year he spends about $3000 on make-up experts who can help him achieve some privacy in public.

"It sounds very strange to some people," he conceded, "but if you were in my shoes and you understood what it is like for me, then you might do the same thing yourself. . . ."

—*Gay Talese,* journalist

So when the woman saw that the tree was good for food, and that it was a delight to the eyes, and that the tree was to be desired to make one wise, she took of its fruit and ate; and she also gave some to her husband, and he ate. Then the eyes of both were opened, and they knew that they were naked; and they sewed fig leaves together and made themselves aprons. And they heard the sound of the Lord God among the trees of the garden in the cool of the day, and the man and his wife hid themselves from the presence of the Lord God among the trees of the garden. But the Lord God called to the man, and said to him, "Where are you?" And he said, "I heard the sound of thee in the garden, and I was afraid, because I was naked; and I hid myself."

—*Genesis 3:6-10*

But I am a worm and no man;
   scorned by men, and despised by the people.
All who see me mock at me,
   they make mouths at me, they wag their heads. . . .

Be not far from me,
   for trouble is near and there is none to help.
Many bulls encompass me,
   strong bulls of Bashan surround me;
They open wide their mouths at me,
   like a ravening and roaring lion.
I am poured out like water,
   and all my bones are out of joint;
My heart is like wax;
   it is melted within my breast;
My strength is dried up like a potsherd,
   and my tongue cleaves to my jaws;
   thou dost lay me in the dust of death.

—*Psalm 22:6,7,11-15*

"Simon, Simon, behold, Satan demanded to have you, that he might sift you like wheat, but I have prayed for you that your faith may not fail; and when you have turned again, strengthen your brethren." And he said to him, "Lord, I am ready to go with you to prison and to death." He said, "I tell you, Peter, the cock will not crow this day, until you three times deny that you know me. . . ." Then they seized him and led him away, bringing him into the high priest's house. Peter followed at a distance; and when they had kindled a fire in the middle of the courtyard and sat down together, Peter sat among them. Then a maid, seeing him as he sat in the light and gazing at him, said, "This man also was with him." But he denied it, saying, "Woman, I do not know him." And a little later some one else saw him and said, "You also are one of them." But Peter said, "Man, I am not." And after an interval of about an hour still another insisted, saying, "Certainly this man also was with him; for he is a Galilean." But Peter said, "Man, I do not know what you are saying." And immediately, while he was still speaking, the cock crowed. And the Lord turned and looked at Peter. . . . And he went out and wept bitterly.

—*Luke 22:31–34,54–62* (incomplete)

I can't face the person I have let down.
I hide behind small talk,
   or big talk;
I cover up my shame with jokes
     or silence.
I can't face myself.
I can't face you, Lord.

But you forgave Peter
   when he let you down.
You appeared to him first
   when you rose from the dead.
You accomplished great things through him.

I take heart, Lord.

PLAYBOY: All the films you've made, in one way or another, are about weak men—psychologically, socially, and often sexually impotent. Is that you?

MASTROIANNI: Yes and no. It's part of me; and I think it's part of many other men today. Modern man is not as virile as he used to be. Instead of making things happen, he waits for things to happen to him. He goes with the current. Something in our society has led him to stop fighting, to cease swimming upstream.

PLAYBOY: What is that something?

MASTROIANNI: Doubt, for one thing. Doubt about his place in society, his purpose in life. In my country, for example, I was brought up with the thought of man as the *padrone,* the pillar of the family. I wanted to be a loving, caring, protective man. But now I feel lost; the sensitive man everywhere feels lost. He is no longer *padrone*—either of his own world or of his women.

PLAYBOY: How about American women?

MASTROIANNI: I've never seen so many unhappy, melancholy women. They have liberty—but they are desperate. Poor darlings, they're so hungry for romance that two little words in their ears are enough to crumble them before your eyes. American women are beautiful, but a little cold and too perfect—too well brought up, with the perfume and the hair always just so and the rose-colored skin. What perfection—and what a bore! Believe me, it makes you want to have a girl with a mustache, crosseyes and runs in her stockings.

I remember my grandfather. He lived to be 90.

I used to watch him and admire his authority. Where has all that gone? What's happened to that kind of man?

Whatever it was that buried him, it took with it a whole era, a whole way of life. It left women doing some of the things he did; and this causes me deep anxiety. But perhaps this is an era in which we *all* feel lost—a period of transition where the only thing that keeps man going is habit. But, here again, women have the advantage. They believe in love, and we men don't even believe in *that* anymore. Once men dueled over women, grand dukes fell at the feet of ballerinas and whole armies chased them. But when a man chases a woman today, we say, "What luck—he can still run." We seem to have forgotten that love can be a most extraordinary support for a man. A man in love is master of the world. Even though love costs him pain, it's a marvelous kind of suffering.

PLAYBOY: Does it have to cause suffering?

MASTROIANNI: Yes. And it almost always ends the same: with disenchantment. The exception is rare, rare.

PLAYBOY: Still, your friends say that you fall in love easily.

MASTROIANNI: That's true—but only on the level of fantasy. In my imagination, I work myself up to a fantastic and sublime passion for a woman. Then I go out with her. But since I've created such an extraordinary love in my mind—which isn't real and exists only within myself—I soon realize she isn't exceptional after all. Then I get tired and go looking for another one. You understand? I've always felt I lacked the capabilities of real, serious love. For me, it's always a game in which I *pretend* to love.

—*Marcello Mastroianni,* actor

My beloved speaks and says to me:
"Arise, my love, my fair one,
  and come away;
for lo, the winter is past,
  the rain is over and gone.
The flowers appear on the earth,
  the time of singing has come,
and the voice of the turtledove
  is heard in our land.
The fig tree puts forth its figs,
  and the vines are in blossom;
  they give forth fragrance.
Arise, my love, my fair one,
  and come away.
O my dove, in the clefts of the rock,
  in the covert of the cliff,
let me see your face,
  let me hear your voice,
for your voice is sweet,
  and your face is comely.
Catch us the foxes,
  the little foxes,
that spoil the vineyards,
  for our vineyards are in blossom."
                    —*Song of Solomon 2:10–15*

. . . for love is strong as death,
  jealousy is cruel as the grave.
Its flashes are flashes of fire,
  a most vehement flame.
Many waters cannot quench love,
  neither can floods drown it.
If a man offered for love
  all the wealth of his house,
  it would be utterly scorned.
                    —*Song of Solomon 8:6b,7*

Love is patient; love is kind and envies no one.
Love is never boastful, nor conceited, nor rude;
  never selfish, nor quick to take offence.
Love keeps no score of wrongs; does not gloat over
  other men's sins, but delights in the truth.
There is nothing love cannot face; there is no limit to its
  faith, its hope, and its endurance.

Love will never come to an end.
                    —I Corinthians 13:4–8 (NEB)

  Lord, I am wondering.
    Am I a weak man, as Mastroianni says?
    Is habit all that keeps me going?

    Do I believe in love, anymore,
      or do I just pretend?
    What is love anyway?
    There's the love that ends in disenchantment.
    There's the love that never ends.

    One thing I know:
      your love for me never ends.

24 *What Can You Do for Me?*

COMMENT: To most of us, a job is merely the money it pays, and money—to most of us—means the acquisition of things. So we trade our time—our life—for money. In the process we tend to judge a man —and he tends to judge himself—not by what he does but by how much money he makes. The trouble is, this leads us to think of everything in terms of commodities. . . . In this mercantile world, everything is for sale, and a person becomes valuable to you for what he can do for you.

GIRL: We're in Love.

BOY: And we're going to get married, no matter what anybody says.

BOTH: But we don't want a big wedding.

GIRL: We just want to slip away together. . . .

COMMENT: Fat chance.

BRIDE'S FATHER: I think John's foolish to want to be a teacher; there's no money in that—how could he support my daughter? I'll find him a place in my business if you can't get him to go to work for you. . . . After all, we should be proud of him.

BRIDE'S MOTHER: Reception, caterer, country club, Cadillacs. Everybody will talk about it! It'll cost a fortune?

BRIDE'S FATHER: Ehh—don't worry. If I invite all my customers, we can take it off the income tax. Besides, it's for the kid. It's the only wedding she'll ever have.

GROOM'S MOTHER: Your Betty said she wanted a simple wedding.

[*They all laugh loudly*]

COMMENT: When we are not thinking of one another in terms of commodities or market values, we tend to think of one another as players of roles. . . . Home sweet home!

HUSBAND: Thank God it's Friday . . . all I want to do is just unwind.

WIFE: I've been waiting for the weekend too. . . . That lawn's a mess . . . and there are those shelves you promised to build in the kitchen . . . and oh . . . that leaky faucet. . . .

HUSBAND: All right . . . all right . . . but this weekend how about a little time for us? We'll get a baby sitter and head for the mountains. . . . How about it honey . . . ? Just the two of us.

WIFE: But sweetheart, we really shouldn't. . . . After all, you're the man of the house and I'm the lady of the house. . . . I want you to straighten up the garage. . . .

COMMENT: She is not listening to him. She is not even talking to him, nor he to her. She is talking to a presumption, not to a human being. She presumes him to be Mr. Fixit, which is presumably the role of the husband. He presumes she is just his little playmate. . . . If we have difficulty in becoming truly involved with one another within our own families, how can we possibly feel a kinship with those millions of total strangers with whose lives our own lives are inextricably bound up? The essential problem is that we live closely together without meeting.

—*John Keats*, writer

When the people saw that Moses delayed to come down from the mountain, the people gathered themselves together to Aaron, and said to him, "Up, make us gods, who shall go before us; as for this Moses, the man who brought us up out of the land of Egypt, we do not know what has become of him." And Aaron said to them, "Take off the rings of gold which are in the ears of your wives, your sons, and your daughters, and bring them to me. . . ." And he received the gold at their hand, and fashioned it with a graving tool, and made a molten calf; and they said, "These are your gods, O Israel, who brought you up out of the land of Egypt! . . ." And the people sat down to eat and drink, and rose up to play. . . . And the Lord said to Moses, "Go down; for your people whom you brought up out of the land of Egypt, have corrupted themselves. . . ." And Moses turned, and went down from the mountain with the two tables of the testimony in his hands. . . . And as soon as he came near the camp and saw the calf and the dancing, Moses' anger burned hot, and he threw the tables out of his hands and broke them at the foot of the mountain. And he took the calf which they had made, and burnt it with fire, and ground it to powder, and scattered it upon the water, and made the people of Israel drink it. And Moses said to Aaron, "What did this people do to you that you have brought a great sin upon them?" And Aaron said, "Let not the anger of my lord burn hot; you know the people, that they are set on evil. For they said to me, 'Make us gods, who shall go before us; as for this Moses, the man who brought us out of the land of Egypt, we do not know what has become of him.' And I said to them, 'Let any who have gold take it off'; so they gave it to me, and I threw it into the fire, and there came out this calf. . . ." Moses said to the people, "You have sinned a great sin. And now I will go up to the Lord; perhaps I can make atonement for your sin." So Moses returned to the Lord and said, "Alas, this people have sinned a great sin; they have made for themselves gods of gold. But now, if thou wilt forgive their sin—and if not, blot me, I pray thee, out of thy book which thou hast written."

—*Exodus 32:1-35* (incomplete)

And James and John, the sons of Zebedee, came forward to him and said to him, "Teacher, we want you to do for us whatever we ask of you." And he said to them, "What do you want me to do for you?" And they said to him, "Grant us to sit, one at your right hand and one at your left, in your glory." But Jesus said to them, "You do not know what you are asking. Are you able to drink the cup that I drink, or to be baptized with the baptism with which I am baptized?" And they said to him, "We are able." And Jesus said to them, "The cup that I drink you will drink; and with the baptism with which I am baptized, you will be baptized; but to sit at my right hand or at my left is not mine to grant, but it is for those for whom it has been prepared." And when the ten heard it, they began to be indignant at James and John. And Jesus called them to him and said to them, "You know that those who are supposed to rule over the Gentiles lord it over them, and their great men exercise authority over them. But it shall not be so among you; but whoever would be great among you must be your servant, and whoever would be first among you must be slave of all. . . ."

—*Mark 10:35-44*

I am like James and John.
Lord, I size up other people
   in terms of what they can do for me;
   how they can further my program,
         feed my ego,
         satisfy my needs,
         give me strategic advantage.

I exploit people,
            ostensibly for your sake,
            but really for my own sake.
    Lord, I turn to you
        to get the inside track
        and obtain special favors,
            your direction for my schemes,
            your power for my projects,
            your sanction for my ambitions,
            your blank check for whatever I want.
I am like James and John.

        Change me, Lord.
        Make me a man who asks of you and of others,
                what can I do for you?

25 *A Secret Debt and a Raised Hat*

When I was brought down from my prison to the Court of Bankruptcy, between two policemen,——— waited in the long dreary corridor that, before the whole crowd, whom an action so sweet and simple hushed into silence, he might gravely raise his hat to me, as, handcuffed and with bowed head, I passed him by. Men have gone to heaven for smaller things than that. It was in this spirit, and with this mode of love, that the saints knelt down to wash the feet of the poor, or stooped to kiss the leper on the cheek. I have never said one single word to him about what he did. I do not know to the present moment whether he is aware that I was even conscious of his action. It is not a thing for which one can render formal thanks in formal words. I store it in the treasure-house of my heart. I keep it there as a secret debt that I am glad to think I can never possibly repay. . . . When wisdom has been profitless to me, philosophy barren, and the proverbs and phrases of those who have sought to give me consolation as dust and ashes in my mouth, the memory of that little, lovely, silent act of love has unsealed for me all the wells of pity, . . . and brought me out of the bitterness of lonely exile into harmony with the wounded, broken, and great heart of the world.

—*Oscar Wilde,* author

But Zion said, "The Lord has forsaken me,
    my Lord has forgotten me."
Can a woman forget her sucking child,
    that she should have no compassion
        on the son of her womb?

Even these may forget,
   yet I will not forget you.
Behold I have graven you on the palms of my hands. . . .
                       —*Isaiah 49:14–16a*

The scribes and Pharisees brought a woman who had been caught in adultery, and placing her in the midst, they said to him, "Teacher, this woman has been caught in the act of adultery. Now in the law Moses commanded us to stone such. What do you say about her?" This they said to test him. Jesus bent down and wrote with his finger on the ground. And as they continued to ask him, he stood up and said to them, "Let him who is without sin among you be the first to throw a stone at her." And once more he bent down and wrote with his finger on the ground. But when they heard it, they went away, one by one, beginning with the eldest, and Jesus was left alone with the woman standing before him. Jesus looked up and said to her, "Woman, where are they? Has no one condemned you?" She said, "No one, Lord." And Jesus said, "Neither do I condemn you; go, and do not sin again."
                       —*John 8:3–11*

Lord, thank you for not condemning me
   when everyone else was pointing the finger at me.

   Let me never forget that your love for me
      has no conditions,
      that I am never forsaken,
      for you are always with me.
   Give me the courage and kindness to raise my hat
      publicly to those I know,
      who suffer defeat, failure, shame.
   Lord, thank you for not condemning me
      when everyone else was pointing the finger at me

26 *Making Love and Breaking Bread*

In spite of everything, there was in the life I fled a zest and a joy and a capacity for facing and surviving disaster that are very moving and very rare. Perhaps we were, all of us—pimps, whores, racketeers, church members, and children—bound together by the nature of our oppression, the specific and peculiar complex of risks we had to run; if so, within these limits we sometimes achieved with each other a freedom that was close to love. I remember anyway, church suppers, and outings, and, later, after I left the church, rent and waistline parties where rage and sorrow sat in the darkness and did not stir, and we ate and drank and talked and laughed and danced and forgot all about "the man." We had the liquor, the chicken, the music, and each other, and had no need to pretend to be what we were not. This is the freedom that one hears in some gospel songs, for example, and in jazz. In all jazz, and especially in the blues, there is something tart and ironic, authoritative and double-edged. . . .

Only people who have been "down the line," as the song puts it, know what this music is about. I think it was Big Bill Broonzy who used to sing "I Feel So Good," a really joyful song about a man who is on the way to the railroad station to meet his girl. She's coming home. It is the singer's incredibly moving exuberance that makes one realize how leaden the time must have been while she was gone. There is no guarantee that she will stay this time, either, as the singer clearly knows, and in fact, she has not yet actually arrived. Tonight, or tomorrow, or within the next five minutes, he may very well be singing "Lonesome in My Bedroom" or insisting "Ain't we, ain't we going to make it all right? Well if we don't today, we will tomorrow night." White Americans do not understand the depths out of which such an ironic tenacity comes, but they suspect that the force is sensual, and they are terrified of sensuality, and do not any longer understand it. The word "sensual" is not intended to bring to mind quivering dusky maidens or priapic black studs. . . . To be sensual, I think, is to respect and rejoice in the force of life, of life itself, and to be *present* in all that one does, from the effort of making love to the breaking of bread. . . . Something very sinister happens to the people of a country when they begin to distrust their own reactions as deeply as they do here, and become as joyless as they have become.

—*James Baldwin,* author

And it was told King David, "The Lord has blessed the household of Obededom and all that belongs to him, because of the ark of God." So David went and brought up the ark of God from the house of Obededom to the city of David with rejoicing; and when those who bore the ark of the Lord had gone six paces, he sacrificed an ox and a fatling. And David danced before the Lord with all his might; and David was girded with a linen ephod. So David and all the house of Israel brought up the ark of the Lord with shouting, and with the sound of the horn.

As the ark of the Lord came into the city of David, Michal, the daughter of Saul, looked out of the window, and saw King David leaping and dancing before the Lord; and she despised him in her heart. . . . And David blessed the people in the name of the Lord of hosts, and distributed among all the people, the whole multitude of Israel, both men and women, to each a cake of bread, a portion of meat, and a cake of raisins.

Then all the people departed, each to his house And David returned to bless his household. But Michal, the daughter of Saul, came out to meet David, and said, "How the king of Israel honored himself today, uncovering himself today before the eyes of his servants' maids, as one of the vulgar fellows shamelessly uncovers himself!" And David said to Michal, "It was before the Lord, who chose me above your father, and above all his house, to appoint me as prince over Israel, the people of the Lord—and I will make merry before the Lord. . . ."

—*II Samuel 6:12–21* (incomplete)

How can I describe this generation? They are like the children sitting in the market-place and shouting at each other,

"We piped for you and you would not dance."

"We wept and wailed, and you would not mourn." For John came, neither eating nor drinking, and they say, "He is possessed." The Son of Man came eating and drinking, and they say, "Look at him! a glutton and a drinker. . . ."

—*Matthew 11:16–19* (NEB) (incomplete)

They met constantly to hear the apostles teach, and to share the common life, to break bread, and to pray. A sense of awe was everywhere, and many marvels and signs were brought about through the apostles. All whose faith had drawn them together held everything in common; they would sell their property and possessions and make a general distribution as the need of each required. With one mind they kept up their daily attendance at the temple, and, breaking bread in private houses, shared their meals with unaffected joy, as they praised God. . . .

—*Acts 2:42–47a* (NEB)

I love this life!
I want to live it to the full.
    Don't let me miss anything good,
    nor scorn those who find what I have missed.

Lord, give me freedom
    to rejoice in your gifts of life and love,
    to be present in all that I do,
    and to praise you with all my strength.

27 *Not to Be Paid Back, but Passed On*

The conductor called, "All visitors off the train!" "Oh David . . ." She hugged him to her bosom which smelled of fruits and vegetables and a mother's love. "Take care of him." These last words were addressed not to Uncle Asher nor even to the conductor, but to God. Tante Dvorah spoke to Him freely and often, for the Lord, to her way of thinking, was a person-sitter to whom loved ones were safely to be entrusted, as well as her senior partner in the business of living, always accessible and invariably amenable to petitions of love.

David looked at his aunt and uncle—she, with hands chapped and hard from selling fruit and vegetables outdoors in all kinds of weather, the face ruddy and round and invariably smiling, the heavy body more accustomed to half a dozen sweaters at one time than a single coat, the hair the color of moonlight now, but the dark eyes still bright; he, with his slight wiry body strong and bent from lifting too many fruit and vegetable crates for too many years, the wind-burned skin, the swarthy face impassive except for the wry mouth— the childless couple who had taken the orphaned David into their home, rearing him since the age of seven yet refusing to be called "Mama" and "Papa" for fear that he would forget his real parents.

David grabbed their rough peddlers' hands in his smooth student ones. "How can I ever begin to repay you two for what you've done for me!" Uncle Asher spoke gently: "David, there's a saying: 'The love of parents goes to their children, but the love of these children goes to *their* children.'"

"That's not so!" David protested. "I'll always be trying to—" Tante Dvorah interrupted. "David, what

your Uncle Asher means is that a parent's love isn't to be paid back; it can only be passed on."
—*Herbert Tarr, author*

Bless the Lord, O my soul;
    and all that is within me, bless his holy name!
Bless the Lord, O my soul,
    and forget not all his benefits,
who forgives all your iniquity,
who heals all your diseases,
who redeems your life from the Pit,
    who crowns you with steadfast love and mercy,
who satisfies you with good as long as you live
    so that your youth is renewed like the eagle's. . . .
The Lord is merciful and gracious,
    slow to anger and abounding in steadfast love.
He will not always chide,
    nor will he keep his anger for ever.
He does not deal with us according to our sins,
    nor requite us according to our iniquities.
For as the heavens are high above the earth,
    so great is his steadfast love toward those who
        fear him;
as far as the east is from the west,
    so far does he remove our transgressions from us.
As a father pities his children,
    so the Lord pities those who fear him.
—*Psalm 103:1–5,8–13*

During supper, Jesus . . . rose from table, laid aside his garments, and taking a towel, tied it round him. Then he poured water into a basin, and began to wash his disciples' feet and to wipe them with the towel. . . . After washing their feet and taking his garments again, he sat down. "Do you understand," he asked, "what I have done for you? You call me 'Master' and 'Lord,'

and rightly so, for that is what I am. Then if I, your
Lord and Master, have washed your feet, you also ought
to wash one another's feet. I have set you an example:
you are to do as I have done for you. . . . I give you a
new commandment: love one another; as I have loved
you, so you are to love one another. . . ."
—*John 13:3–5* (incomplete), *12–15,34* (NEB)

Lord, thank you for those who
   have washed my feet in a hundred ways,
   especially———
   and———.

Thank you for your love for me.
   It shames me.
   I am grateful.

Help me to pass on your love today,
   to those closest to me,
   to those estranged from me.

The idea that comes most naturally to man, as if from his very nature, is the idea of his innocence. . . . Each of us insists on being innocent at all cost, even if he has to accuse the whole human race and heaven itself. You won't delight a man by complimenting him on the efforts by which he has become intelligent or generous. On the other hand, he will beam if you admire his natural generosity. Inversely, if you tell a criminal that his crime is not due to his nature or his character but to unfortunate circumstances, he will be extravagantly grateful to you. . . . It's a matter of dodging judgment. Since it is hard to dodge it, tricky to get one's nature simultaneously admired and excused, they all strive to be rich. Why? Did you ever ask yourself? For power, of course. But especially because wealth shields from immediate judgment, takes you out of the subway crowd to enclose you in a chromium-plated automobile, isolates you in huge protected lawns, Pullmans, first-class cabins. Wealth, *cher ami,* is not quite acquittal, but reprieve, and that's always worth taking.

Above all, don't believe your friends when they ask you to be sincere with them. They merely hope you will encourage them in the good opinion they have of themselves by providing them with the additional assurance they will find in your promise of sincerity. How could sincerity be a condition of friendship? A liking for truth at any cost is a passion that spares nothing and that nothing resists. It's a vice, at times a comfort, or a selfishness. Therefore, if you are in that situation, don't hesitate: promise to tell the truth and then lie as best you can. You will satisfy their hidden desire and doubly prove your affection.

This is so true that we rarely confide in those who are better than we. Rather, we are more inclined to flee their society. Most often, on the other hand, we confess to those who are like us and who share our weaknesses. Hence we don't want to improve ourselves or be bettered, for we should first have to be judged in default. We merely wish to be pitied and encouraged in the course we have chosen. In short we should like, at the same time, to cease being guilty and yet not to make the effort of cleansing ourselves. Not enough cynicism and not enough virtue. We lack the energy of evil as well as the energy of good. . . .

However that may be, after prolonged research on myself, I brought out the fundamental duplicity of the human being. Then I realized, as a result of delving into my memory, that modesty helped me to shine, humility to conquer, and virtue to oppress. . . .

And why should I change, since I have found the happiness that suits me? I have accepted duplicity instead of being upset about it. . . .

—*Albert Camus,* author

Transgression speaks to the wicked
    deep in his heart;
there is no fear of God
    before his eyes.
For he flatters himself in his own eyes
    that his iniquity cannot be found out and hated.
The words of his mouth are mischief and deceit;
    he has ceased to act wisely and do good.
He plots mischief while on his bed;
    he sets himself in a way that is not good;
    he spurns not evil.

—*Psalm 36:1–4*

. . . do you imagine . . . that you . . . will escape the judgement of God? Or do you think lightly of his wealth of kindness, of tolerance, and of patience, without recognizing that God's kindness is meant to lead you to a change of heart? In the rigid obstinacy of your heart you are laying up for yourself a store of retribution for the day of retribution, when God's just judgement will be revealed, and . . . those who pursue glory, honour, and immortality by steady persistence in well-doing, he will give eternal life; but for those who are governed by selfish ambition, who refuse obedience to the truth and take the wrong for their guide, there will be the fury of retribution . . . on the day when God judges the secrets of human hearts through Christ Jesus.

—Romans 2:3–8,16 (NEB)

Now there is in Jerusalem by the Sheep Gate a pool, in Hebrew called Bethzatha, which has five porticoes. In these lay a multitude of invalids, blind, lame, paralyzed. One man was there who had been ill for thirty-eight years. When Jesus saw him and knew that he had been lying there for a long time, he said to him, "Do you want to be healed?"

—John 5:2–6

I have knowingly and willingly disobeyed you, Lord,
  counting on your forgiveness all the while.

Yet, I know that I cannot dodge your judgment.
  I know some choices have to be made.
  I have to decide what I want most.

Lord, I want to want to be healed.

View from the Bottom of the Well

... It was a long village, stretching along both sides of the road, and at the centre we found a crowd of people surrounded by soldiers with their weapons raised—bearded peasants in worn boots and dirty caps, brawny women with shawls over their heads, and girls in over-short skirts. ... There were no men of military age. The people were all on their knees, their voices wailing in chorus, their arms raised in supplication. ...

He gasped in my ear: "Sebastian, what are they up to? What are they doing? Have they gone mad?" I didn't answer. They weren't mad, they were carrying out orders; and the people who had given the orders weren't mad either, but were pursuing a logic that was entirely scientific and rational. ... Since we could not leave these deep wells for the use of the oncoming enemy, and since neither explosives nor sappers were available, we were filling them up with the village population, shooting them on the edge or pushing them in alive.

... As Romeo and I hurried out of the village ... we heard bursts of machine gun fire behind us ... "Well, what do you think of that?" I said maliciously to Romeo. ... "We couldn't save them," said Romeo, breathing with difficulty. "If we'd tried to interfere those bloody gendarmes would have arrested us and we'd probably have been shot ourselves. There was nothing we could do. ... After all ... we do our duty, and that's all we have to do. We aren't responsible for—for things like that." For some moments I said nothing. Then I asked myself aloud: "Are any of them still alive? The people in that well—perhaps there's one left, somewhere in the middle, not dead yet. But there must be too many on top of him for him to have a hope of getting out." "Well, and what do you want me to do about it?" cried Romeo in anguish. "Who am I, anyway? Why should I try to save them? Do it yourself, if you think you can!"

... A truck packed with soldiers drove past at high speed, smothering us in dust: they were the men of the field-police who had filled up the well. "Do you believe in God?" I asked Romeo ... as he stared after it. He replied doggedly, "Yes."

—*Petru Dumitriu,* author

Deep calls to deep
   at the thunder of thy cataracts;
all thy waves and billows
   have gone over me.
By day the Lord commands his steadfast love:
   and at night his song is with me,
   a prayer to the God of my life.
I say to God, my rock;
   "Why hast thou forgotten me?
Why go I mourning
   because of the oppression of the enemy?"
As with a deadly wound in my body,
   my adversaries taunt me,
while they say to me continually,
   "Where is thy God?"

—*Psalm 42:7-10*

And at the ninth hour Jesus cried with a loud voice ... "My God, my God, why hast thou forsaken me?"

—*Mark 15:34*

From out of the city the dying groan,
and the soul of the wounded cries for help;
yet God pays no attention to their prayer.

—*Job 24:12*

[99]

But now thus says the Lord,
  he who created you, O Jacob,
  he who formed you, O Israel:
Fear not, for I have redeemed you:
  I have called you by name, you are mine.
When you pass through the waters I will be with you:
  and through the rivers, they shall not overwhelm you:
when you walk through fire you shall not be burned,
  and the flame shall not consume you.
For I am the Lord your God,
  the Holy One of Israel, your Savior.
I give Egypt as your ransom,
  Ethiopia and Seba in exchange for you.
Because you are precious in my eyes,
  and honored, and I love you,
I give men in return for you,
  peoples in exchange for your life.
Fear not, for I am with you;
  I will bring your offspring from the east,
  and from the west I will gather you;
I will say to the north, Give up,
  and to the south, Do not withhold;
bring my sons from afar
  and my daughters from the end of the earth,
every one who is called by my name,
  whom I created for my glory,
  whom I formed and made.

—*Isaiah 43:1-7*

O God, how can you stand what happened at that well?
Why do you allow that kind of thing in your world?
What possible meaning is there in it?

Yet, you gave up your Son to suffer and die,
        helpless and forsaken,

for the sake of all the people in all the wells,
for my sake.

I know you care, Lord.
Help me to believe that I and all men
        are precious to you.
Help me to believe in you,
        when I cannot understand your ways.
Lord, I believe. Help my unbelief.

30 *Yes*

. . . we were at work in a trench. The dawn was gray around us; gray was the sky above; gray the snow in the pale light of dawn; gray the rags in which my fellow prisoners were clad, and gray their faces. . . . I was struggling to find the *reason* for my sufferings, my slow dying. In a last violent protest against the hopelessness of imminent death, I sensed my spirit piercing through the enveloping gloom. I felt it transcend that hopeless, meaningless world, and from somewhere I heard a victorious "Yes" in answer to my question of the existence of an ultimate purpose. At that moment a light was lit in a distant farmhouse, which stood on the horizon as if painted there, in the midst of the miserable gray of a dawning morning in Bavaria. "Et lux in tenebris lucet"—and the light shineth in the darkness.

—*Viktor Frankl,* psychiatrist

I don't know Who—or what—put the question, I don't know when it was put. I don't even remember answering. But at some moment I did answer *Yes* to Someone—or Something—and from that hour I was certain that existence is meaningful and that, therefore, my life, in self-surrender, had a goal. From that moment I have known what it means "not to look back," and "to take no thought for the morrow."

—*Dag Hammarskjold,* statesman

Now Moses was keeping the flock of his father-in-law, Jethro, the priest of Midian; and he led his flock to the west side of the wilderness, and came to Horeb, the mountain of God. And the angel of the Lord appeared to him in a flame of fire out of the midst of a bush; and he looked, and lo, the bush was burning, yet it was not consumed. And Moses said, "I will turn aside and see this great sight, why the bush is not burnt." When the Lord saw that he turned aside to see, God called to him out of the bush, "Moses, Moses!" And he said, "Here am I." Then he said, "Do not come near; put off your shoes from your feet, for the place on which you are standing is holy ground." And he said, "I am the God of your father, the God of Abraham, the God of Isaac, and the God of Jacob." And Moses hid his face, for he was afraid to look at God. . . . Then Moses said to God, "If I come to the people of Israel and say to them, 'The God of your fathers has sent me to you,' and they ask me, 'What is his name?' what shall I say to them?" God said to Moses, "I AM WHO I AM." And he said, "Say this to the people of Israel, 'I AM has sent me to you.'"

—Exodus 3:1–6,13,14

As they were going along the road, a man said to him, "I will follow you wherever you go." And Jesus said to him, "Foxes have holes, and birds of the air have nests; but the Son of man has nowhere to lay his head." To another he said, "Follow me." But he said, "Lord, let me first go and bury my father." But he said to him, "Leave the dead to bury the dead; but as for you, go and proclaim the kingdom of God." Another said, "I will follow you, Lord; but first let me say farewell to those at my home." Jesus said to him, "No one who puts his hand to the plow and looks back is fit for the kingdom of God."

—Luke 9:57–62

My hopes have been disappointed again.
My frustration is making me bitter.

I'm not getting anywhere.
What do I do next?
What *can* I do?
Answer me, Lord.

Give me faith to recognize your Yes when
   it comes to me
   at my cluttered desk,
   while I sip my coffee
      and watch the children fight and play,
   as I make out my expense account
      and the agenda for tonight's meeting,
   as I worry about the repairs needed on the house
      and the car,
      college costs,
      and retirement. . . .

Lord, give me courage **to tr**ust my hunches,
   and patience to take one step at a time.
I belong to you.
I will walk with you.
Yes.

STARBUCK, the dreamer of dreams that almost never come true, complains to Lizzie about a world in which reality falls far short of a man's vision.

STARBUCK: ... Nothing's as pretty in your hands as it was in your head. There ain't no world near as good as the world I got up here (*angrily tapping his forehead*). Why?

LIZZIE: I don't know. Maybe it's because you don't take time to see it. Always on the go—here, there, nowhere. Running away . . . keeping your own company. Maybe if you'd keep company with the *world* . . .

STARBUCK: (*doubtfully*) I'd learn to love it?

LIZZIE: You might—if you saw it *real*. Some nights I'm in the kitchen washing the dishes. And Pop's playing poker with the boys. Well, I'll watch him real close. And at first I'll just see an ordinary middle-aged man—not very interesting to look at. And then, minute by minute, I'll see little things I never saw in him before. Good things and bad things—queer little habits I never noticed he had—and ways of talking I never paid any mind to. And suddenly I know who he is—and I love him so much I could cry! And I want to thank God I took the time to see him real.

—*N. Richard Nash,* playwright

And a great storm of wind arose, and the waves beat into the boat, so that the boat was already filling. But he was in the stern, asleep on the cushion; and they woke him and said to him, "Teacher, do you not care if we perish?" And he awoke and rebuked the wind, and said to the sea, "Peace! Be still!" and the wind ceased, and there was a great calm. He said to them, "Why are you afraid? Have you no faith?" And they were filled with awe, and said to one another, "Who then is this, that even wind and sea obey him?"

... And Jesus went on with his disciples, to the villages of Caesarea Philippi; and on the way he asked his disciples, "Who do men say that I am?" And they told him, "John the Baptist; and others say, Elijah; and others one of the prophets." And he asked them, "But who do you say that I am?"

... And Pilate asked him, "Are you the King of the Jews?"

—Mark 4:37–41; 8:27–29a; 15:2a

That very day two of them were going to a village named Emmaus, about seven miles from Jerusalem, and talking with each other about all these things that had happened. While they were talking and discussing together, Jesus himself drew near and went with them. But their eyes were kept from recognizing him. . . . So they drew near to the village to which they were going. He appeared to be going further, but they constrained him, saying, "Stay with us, for it is toward evening and the day is now far spent." So he went in to stay with them. When he was at table with them, he took the bread and blessed, and broke it, and gave it to them. And their eyes were opened and they recognized him.

—Luke 24:13–16,28–31a

For the love of Christ leaves us no choice, when once we have reached the conclusion that one man

died for all and therefore all mankind has died. His purpose in dying for all was that men, while still in life, should cease to live for themselves, and should live for him who for their sake died and was raised to life. From now on, therefore, we regard no one from a human point of view; even though we once regarded Christ from a human point of view, we regard him thus no longer. When anyone is united to Christ, there is a new world. . . .
        —*II Corinthians 5:14–17* (NEB); (*vs. 16* RSV)

I pray that your inward eyes may be illumined, so that you may know what is the hope to which he calls you. . . .
                        —*Ephesians 1:18* (NEB)

> My eyes are squinting, Lord.
> I'm looking for you
>   in the restaurant,
>   during the coffee break,
>   across the supper table.
>
> Are you looking at me
>   through the eyes of that waiter,
>   in the frown of my secretary,
>   in the smile of my daughter?
> My eyes are squinting, Lord.

Perhaps it is easy for those who have never felt the stinging darts of segregation to say, "Wait." But when you have seen vicious mobs lynch your mothers and fathers at will and drown your sisters and brothers at whim; when you have seen hate-filled policemen curse, kick and even kill your black brothers and sisters; when you see the vast majority of your twenty million Negro brothers smothering in an airtight cage of poverty in the midst of an affluent society; when you suddenly find your tongue twisted and your speech stammering as you seek to explain to your six-year-old daughter why she can't go to the public amusement park that has just been advertised on television, and see tears welling up in her eyes when she is told that Funtown is closed to colored children, and see ominous clouds of inferiority beginning to form in her little mental sky, and see her beginning to distort her personality by developing an unconscious bitterness toward white people; when you have to concoct an answer for a five-year-old son who is asking: "Daddy, why do white people treat colored people so mean?"; when you take a cross-country drive and find it necessary to sleep night after night in the uncomfortable corners of your automobile because no motel will accept you; when you are humiliated day in and day out by nagging signs reading "white" and "colored"; when your first name becomes "nigger," your middle name becomes "boy" (however old you are) and your last name becomes "John," and your wife and mother are never given the respected title "Mrs."; when you are harried by day and haunted by night by the fact that you are a Negro, living constantly at tiptoe stance, never quite knowing what to expect next, and are plagued with inner fears and outer resentments; when you are forever fighting a degenerating sense of "nobodiness"—then you will understand why we find it difficult to wait.

—*Martin Luther King,* minister

The Spirit of the Lord is upon me
  because the Lord has anointed me
to bring good tidings to the afflicted;
  he has sent me to bind up the brokenhearted,
to proclaim liberty to the captives,
  and the opening of the prison to those who are bound;
to proclaim the year of the Lord's favor,
  and the day of vengeance of our God;
to comfort all who mourn;
to grant to those who mourn in Zion—
  to give them a garland instead of ashes,
the oil of gladness instead of mourning,
  the mantle of praise instead of a faint spirit;
that they may be called oaks of righteousness,
  the planting of the Lord, that he may be glorified.
  . . . For I the Lord love justice,
    I hate robbery and wrong.
      —*Isaiah 61:1–3,8* (see also *Luke 4:16–21*)

Finally then, find your strength in the Lord, in his mighty power. Put on all the armour which God provides, so that you may be able to stand firm against the devices of the devil. For our fight is not against human foes, but against cosmic powers, against the authorities and potentates of this dark world. . . .

Therefore, take up God's armour; then you will be able to stand your ground when things are at their worst, to complete every task and still to stand. Stand

firm, I say. Buckle on the belt of truth; for coat of
mail put on integrity; let the shoes on your feet be
the gospel of peace, to give you firm footing; and,
with all these take up the great shield of faith, with
which you will be able to quench all the flaming
arrows of the evil one. Take salvation for helmet;
for sword, take that which the Spirit gives you—the
words that come from God. Give yourselves wholly
to prayer and entreaty; pray on every occasion in the
power of the Spirit. To this end keep watch and
persevere, always interceding for all God's people; and
pray for me, that I may be granted the right words
when I open my mouth, and may boldly and freely
make known his hidden purpose, for which I am an
ambassador—in chains. Pray that I may speak of it
boldly, as it is my duty to speak.

—*Ephesians 6:10–20*

O God, make me love justice,
    and seek equal job opportunity where I work,
    open housing in my apartment building or suburb,
    open membership in my club,
        better schools for all children in my city.

O God, make me hate wrong,
    and speak out against it boldly,
    at parties,
    among my relatives,
    in my church board meetings,
    at work.

O God, keep me from being contentious,
    but make me care enough to contend
        for justice,
        against wrong,
            with humility.

33 *Reading Your Own Obituary*

One morning in 1888, Nobel, inventor of dynamite, the man who had spent his life amassing a fortune from the manufacture and sale of weapons of destruction, awoke to read his own obituary. The obituary was printed as a result of a simple journalistic error—Alfred's brother had died, and a French reporter carelessly reported the death of the wrong brother. Any man would be disturbed under the circumstances, but to Alfred Nobel the shock was overwhelming. He saw himself as the world saw him —"the dynamite King," the great industrialist who had made an immense fortune from explosives. This —as far as the general public was concerned—was the entire purpose of his life. None of his true intentions—to break down the barriers that separated men and ideas—were recognized or given serious consideration. He was quite simply a merchant of death, and for that alone would he be remembered. . . . As he read his obituary with horror, Nobel resolved to make clear to the world the true meaning and purpose of his life. This could be done through the final disposition of his fortune. His last will and testament would be the expression of his life's ideals. . . . The result was the most valued of prizes given to those who have done most for the cause of world peace.

—*Nicholas Halasz,* author

There was once a rich man, who dressed in purple and the finest linen, and feasted in magnificence every day. At his gate, covered with sores, lay a poor man named Lazarus, who would have been glad to satisfy his hunger with the scraps from the rich man's table. Even the dogs used to come and lick his sores. One day the poor man died and was carried away by the angels to be with Abraham. The rich man also died and was buried, and in Hades, where he was in torment, he looked up; and there, far away, was Abraham with Lazarus close beside him. "Abraham, my father," he called out, "take pity on me! Send Lazarus to dip the tip of his finger in water, to cool my tongue, for I am in agony in this fire." But Abraham said, "Remember, my child, that all the good things fell to you while you were still alive, and all the bad to Lazarus; now he has his consolation here and it is you who are in agony. But that is not all: there is a great chasm fixed between us; no one from our side who wants to reach you can cross it, and none may pass from your side to us."

"Then, father," he replied, "will you send him to my father's house where I have five brothers, to warn them, so that they too may not come to this place of torment?" But Abraham said, "They have Moses and the prophets; let them listen to them."

"No, father Abraham," he replied, "but if someone from the dead visits them, they will repent." Abraham answered, "If they do not listen to Moses and the prophets they will pay no heed even if someone should rise from the dead."

—Luke 16:19-31 (NEB)

He looked up and saw the rich people dropping their gifts into the chest of the temple treasury; and he noticed a poor widow putting in two tiny coins. "I tell you this," he said: "this poor widow has given more than any of them; for those others who have given had more than enough, but she, with less than enough, has given all she had to live on."

—*Luke 21:1-4* (NEB)

Therefore, my brothers, I implore you by God's mercy to offer your very selves to him: a living sacrifice, dedicated and fit for his acceptance, the worship offered by mind and heart. Adapt yourselves no longer to the pattern of this present world, but let your minds be remade and your whole nature thus transformed. Then you will be able to discern the will of God, and to know what is good, acceptable, and perfect.

—*Romans 12:1, 2* (NEB)

> Lord, here is my money.
> Help me discern how you
>   would have me spend it.
> Where am I being extravagant?
>   And where niggardly?
>
> Lord, here is my time.
> Help me sort out my
>   responsibilities.
> What should I say No to?
> What should I say Yes to?
>
> Lord, here I am.

34   *A Cry of Joy*

LOREN EISELEY was on an expedition to capture birds
and reptiles alive for a zoo. He found a cabin which
had been unoccupied for years. The cabin had holes in
the roof through which birds had come to roost in the
rafters. He put a ladder against one of the beams, and
with flashlight ready to blind the birds, he crept up
until head and arms were over the shelf.

I snapped on the flash and sure enough there was
a great beating and feathers flying, but instead of my
having them, they, or rather he, had me. He had
my hand, that is, and for a small hawk not much
bigger than my fist he was doing all right. I heard
him give one short metallic cry when the light went
on and my hand descended on the bird beside him;
after that he was busy with his claws and his beak
was sunk in my thumb. He was a sparrow hawk
and a fine young male in the prime of life. I was
sorry not to catch the pair of them, but as I dripped
blood and folded his wings carefully, holding him
by the back so that he couldn't strike again, I had to
admit the two of them might have been more than I
could have handled under the circumstances. The
little fellow had saved his mate by diverting me, and
that was that. He was born to it, and made no outcry
now, resting in my hand hopelessly, but peering toward me in the shadows behind the lamp with a
fierce, almost indifferent glance. He neither gave nor
expected mercy and something out of the high air
passed from him to me, stirring a faint embarrassment.

* * *

Eiseley put the bird in a small box for the night.
The next morning he brought the box out onto the

grass and prepared to make a cage. He looked up in the deep blue sky of the morning to see if there was any sign of the other little hawk, but she had evidently gone for good. On an impulse, Eiseley took the bird out of the box.

* * *

He lay limp in my grasp and I could feel his heart pound under the feathers, but he only looked beyond me and up. I saw him look that last look away beyond me into a sky so full of light that I could not follow his gaze. . . . I suppose I must have had an idea then of what I was going to do, but I never let it come into consciousness. I just reached over and laid the hawk on the grass.

He lay there a long minute without hope, unmoving, his eyes still fixed on that blue vault above him. It must have been that he was already so far away in heart that he never felt the release from my hand. He never even stood. He just lay with his breast against the grass. In the next second after that long minute he was gone. Like a flicker of light he had vanished with my eyes full on him, but without actually seeing even a premonitory wing beat. He was gone straight into that towering emptiness of light and crystal that my eyes could scarcely bear to penetrate. For another long moment there was silence. I could not see him. The light was too intense. Then from far up somewhere a cry came ringing down.

I was young then and had seen little of the world, but when I heard that cry my heart turned over. It was not the cry of the hawk I had captured; for, by shifting my position against the sun, I was now seeing further up. Straight out of the sun's eye, where she must have been soaring restlessly above us for untold hours, hurtled his mate. . . . I saw them both now. He was rising to meet her. . . . And from far up, ringing from peak to peak of the summits over us, came a cry of such unutterable and ecstatic joy that it sounds down across the years and tingles among the cups on my quiet breakfast table.

—*Loren Eiseley,* anthropologist

Soar we now where Christ has led
Following our exalted head,
Made like him, like him we rise,
Ours the cross, the grave the skies.

—*Charles Wesley*

For the Lord himself will descend from heaven with a cry of command, with the archangel's call, and with the sound of the trumpet of God. And the dead in Christ will rise first; then we who are alive, who are left, shall be caught up together with them in the clouds to meet the Lord in the air; and so we shall always be with the Lord. Therefore comfort one another with these words.

—*I Thessalonians 4:16–18*

O God, thank you for the Resurrection!
Thank you for reunion,
            and reconciliation.
I praise you.
I love you.
I worship you! forever and ever!

Amen.

About the Author

THE REVEREND Dr. Robert A. Raines was born in Newton, Massachusetts, in 1926, grew up in Minneapolis, Minnesota, and spent two years in the Navy before entering Yale University. At Yale, he was president of his senior class and earned varsity letters in football and hockey. Elected to Phi Beta Kappa, he graduated in 1950.

Dr. Raines graduated cum laude from Yale Divinity School in 1953. In 1953-4, he studied at Clare College at Cambridge University, England, on a Fulbright Scholarship. In April of 1971, he received an Honorary Doctor of Humanities Degree at Otterbein College, Westerville, Ohio.

Dr. Raines served as minister of Aldersgate Methodist Church in Cleveland from 1954 to 1961; as co-minister of First United Methodist Church of Germantown in Philadelphia from 1961 to 1970; and as Senior Minister of First Community Church in Columbus, Ohio, from April 1970 until February 1974.

Dr. Raines' committee memberships in recent years have included: Parish Ministers Program Selection Committee of the Fund for Theological Education, Board of Directors of the Fund for Theological Education, University Council of Yale University (Chairman of the Committee on the Divinity School and Department of Religious Studies), Ethics Commission of the State of Ohio (first Chairman).

Dr. Raines is now Director of Kirkridge Retreat and Study Center in Bangor, Pennsylvania. He is the author of nine books.

February, 1977